D1687237

Tinted Trails

Exploring Writings in English as a Second Language

Tinted Trails

Exploring Writings in English as a Second Language

AN ANTHOLOGY BY TINT

EDITED BY
Lisa Schantl, Filippo Bagnasco, Andrea Färber and Chiara Meitz

GUEST EDITORS
Marjorie Agosín and Juhea Kim

CONSULTING EDITORS
Matthew Monroy and John Salimbene

ART CURATOR
Vanesa Erjavec

FORUM STADTPARK

Publisher
FORUM STADTPARK
Stadtpark 1, 8010 Graz
Austria

Cover and Illustrations
Vanesa Erjavec

Layout and Type Setting
Andreas Kolli

Fonts
Nitti Grotesk by Pieter van Rosmalen
Minion 3 by Robert Slimbach

Paper
Inside: Munken Pure 120g
Cover: Via Felt Natural 350g

Printer
Druckwerk6

ISBN
978-3-901109-84-3

© Tint, 2023
Tint – ESL Literary Journal and Association /
Verein für Fremdsprachenliteratur

All rights reserved, including the right to
reproduce this book or portions thereof
in any form whatsoever. For information
address Tint at info@tintjournal.com.

Produced in Austria

Tint Journal is the leading online literary journal for those who write prose and poetry in English as their second or non-native language.

By choosing English as their creative tool, these writers provide an extensive audience with a window into their values, ideas, and beliefs. Coming from a wide variety of backgrounds, they bridge borders and blend cultures, offering the purest and deepest understanding of their fiction and nonfiction worlds.

Over the years, Tint has become a multifaceted platform for emerging and established ESL writers, and it encourages them to embrace their non-native English backgrounds. Their unique linguistic landscapes shape their creative voices and influence their readers' experiences. This quality has been ignored — even shamed — for too long. Through the innovative, *tinted* lenses of ESL writers, Tint shines a light on the ways that authors all over the globe can contribute to what we know as literature in English.

Contents

1	Preface by Lisa Schantl
7	Introduction by Marjorie Agosín
11	Introduction by Juhea Kim

15   BELONGING

18	Introduction by Andrea Färber
20	**Amphibian** by Natalie Bühler
24	**The Liars' Village** by Lindi Dedek
32	**My Azov Sea** by Viktoriia Grivina
40	**Still Life with Deer** by Wil-Lian Guzmanos
48	**The Overcoat** by Leonid Newhouse
60	**The Brother Moves On** by Sihle Ntuli
64	**Cuminte** by Adriana Oniță
66	**Dogs** by Giada Pesce
68	**It's Like a Curry Sandwich** by Skanda Prasad
74	**Sito** by Laura Theis

77   (IM)MIGRATION

80	Introduction by Filippo Bagnasco
82	**No Place Called Home** by Urvashi Bundel
84	**Otherland** by Edvige Giunta
86	**When We First Arrived, 1983** by Gabriela Halas
90	**History Flooding the Continent** by Ioana Morpurgo
92	**Immigrant Sitcom** by Francisco Serrano
96	**The Singing Tree** by Nilofar Shidmehr

105 UPHEAVAL

108 Introduction by Lisa Schantl
110 **Hard Labor: Childbirth Soviet Style** by Galina Chernaya
120 **Snake Baby** by Min "Matthew" Choi
128 **Three Chairs** by Naoko Fujimoto
130 **How We Said Goodbye** by Yanita Georgieva
132 **Into Something Rich and Strange** by Lisa Giacalone
134 **Evenings in Monroe Apartments** by Gladwell Pamba
138 **The River-Song** by Susmita Paul
142 **Two Possibilities for Shylock** by Ilan Stavans
146 **jailmaze** by Maja Ulasik
150 **For Your Own Good** by Huina Zheng

163 IDENTITIES

166 Introduction by Chiara Meitz
168 **The Hijab as a Red Herring** by Leila Aboulela
178 **identity is a territory** by Olja Alvir
180 **A Brief Chronology of My English Accent** by Tim Tim Cheng
184 **An Ode to My Inner Ballerina** by Brianna Colmenares
186 **Coty 24** by Jee Ann Guibone
196 **Can You See?** by Thea Inuk Lønberg-Jensen
200 **from Color(s) of the DAY** by Yuko Otomo
206 **Madness Is a Personal Metaphor** by Akhila Pingali
208 **The River** by Jingshu Yao

219 Biographies
229 Tint Writers
231 Tint Volunteers
233 Kickstarter Campaign Backers
235 Content Warnings
237 List of Illustrations
239 Endnotes

Preface
Lisa Schantl

The idea of *Tint Journal*, of a literary magazine that would lift the curtains for English as a second language (ESL) writers, was born on a sun-swollen day in Los Angeles where I attended the Publishing Workshop by the University of Southern California and the *Los Angeles Review of Books* after my study-year abroad. I remember the glistening cobblestones on the campus of the university, the seminar room drowsy from a packed day with new faces and new terms. When the workshop's staff asked the 2018 cohort on which own projects the individuals wanted to work, I first fell silent. Not because the heat had gotten the better of me and also not because I could not think of anything, but because I suddenly was able to visualize it all. Emotions washed over me: of feeling helpless when put on the spot because of my linguistic and geographical otherness, of foaming inside when realizing that I had received a lower grade than my peers because of the teacher's assumptions about my non-native writing skills, and of the warmth and comfort that poems and stories had gifted me with in these and similar moments—when life seemed to rather eat me whole. I shyly raised my hand.

That was it. Within minutes, I had found peers to work with on a journal for second language literature, and a couple of weeks later the first issue was ready to go live. I will never cease to thank my mentors at the Publishing Workshop for enabling me to act against language discrimination, and my colleagues of the first moments—Kenny, Valeria, Rongqian and Rachel—for drafting a more colorful literary world together with me.

To this day, multi- and translingual literature have remained niche forms of writing. Too often, national borders are equated with language borders,[1] and extraordinary ways of expression are labelled as "the unwanted Other." Yet, languages have been crossing borders throughout human history and "transareal and transcultural origins and effects"[2] have been shaping literature even before its written form came into existence. Writers who choose a language other than the one they acquired first may have different reasons and motivations to do so; what binds them together is their sensitivity for structures and semantics, their passion for creating something new, and the many physical, emotional and verbal memories that shine the brightest when the borders between first and foreign language(s) dissolve.

In ten issues, *Tint Journal* has collected the narratives of translingual writers who choose the English language as their creative voice. English is the world's most spoken second language, with more second than first language speakers.[3] This unique status can be traced back to the colonial power of the British and the economic power of the U.S., allowing English to become a global language of all domains and spaces over the past two centuries.[4] The publishing sector mirrors these developments: The most popular books nowadays are often original creations in English,[5] and countries in which English is intensely promoted as a language for economic and personal growth, such as India, started developing their own English-language publishing markets.[6]

It should come as no surprise that among the almost 1 billion ESL speakers there are some who identify as writers and who have found a viable tool with the English language. With intercultural competence and careful attention to detail, these writers weave their personal roots into their narratives and invite their readers to critically engage with stereotypes, prejudices and language conventions. Letter for letter, they make the language their own and manifest idiosyncratic linguistic landscapes. The resulting diversity of works in English as a second language is incredibly vast, bright and intense; however, it is also far from being exhausted by larger publishing houses — often it is not even explored, let alone encouraged, but rather cast aside.

Tint Journal has set out to change the visibility of ESL writers for the better: So far, our literary magazine has been able to showcase more than 200 emerging and established authors from over 70 different countries in biannual issues. As founder and editor-in-chief, I wish to express my thanks to everyone who has contributed to this project over the past five years — as a writer, as an artist, or as a volunteer. The quality exhibited in the digital pages could neither have been reached nor maintained if it weren't for the excellent submissions with every open call and the dedicated editors from all over the globe who helped me curate and refine the texts, and the word about the magazine would not have traveled that far without passionate marketing assistants. Moreover, as a nonprofit association, Tint has hosted a variety of events such as readings and workshops over the last years, locally in Austria or wherever possible as well as online. Every event involved at least as many helping hands as performing writers, and I want to thank all of them. All ever-published writers and ever-engaged volunteers are credited later in this book.

This anthology, *Tinted Trails*, is our 5-year-anniversary publication to celebrate Tint's achievements in a collaborative effort to contribute to the building of a more open-minded and transcultural literary scene. As far as we know, with its dedication solely to English as a second language writing, this collection is the first of its kind. Following the categories of *Tint Journal*, it holds fiction, nonfiction and poetry by authors who were previously published in the online literary magazine as well as by other well-established translingual writers. The showcased works have been carefully chosen in multiple rounds, with the finale judged by the book's guest editors Marjorie Agosín and Juhea Kim, consulting editors and long-time *Tint Journal* volunteers Matthew Monroy and John Salimbene, and the anthology editors Filippo Bagnasco, Andrea Färber, Chiara Meitz and myself. Another special round involved our readership and followers, and resulted in the decoration of one text with the Readers' Choice Award.

The variety of the cultural, geographical and personal experiences of the authors in this collection acts as a tribute to the diversity of second language writing. It is this diversity that allows us to see the world, its cultures and rituals, in a more nuanced way. In a publication like this one, these nuances are given the chance to stand on their own *and* in relation to each other, and thus will hopefully cue the book's readers to thoughts and discussions about the individual entries as well as their meeting points. Diversity does not only happen on the content level but also on the discourse level: This means that readers will find different standardizations of spelling, different approaches to the accentuation of foreign language words, and also various forms of code-switching and language mixing on the following pages. At Tint, we want to give writers a chance to experiment with translingual modes of expression, rather than forcing one scheme upon everyone. I hope you will find as much pleasure as I do in exploring norms as well as their defiances.

From the first days of this project in the boundless L.A. heat, it was considered the best choice to have *Tint Journal* dwell mainly in the online realm because of its then intended, now vivid international author- and readership. Yet, as someone who still buys physical books, borrows physical copies from the library and loves browsing through physical literary magazines, a tangible, actual book filled to the brim with tinted texts has been a long-held dream of mine. When I posed the idea for a printed anniversary publication to Tint's team members almost two years ago, I received the reaction that I had been hoping for: Most of them had been dreaming of a book to hold, gift and cherish just like me, and they were just as eager as I to start working on it. Now, finally seeing the light of day with the generous patronage of the publishing house FORUM STADTPARK, this book has become much more: It is a token of translingual literature, a testament to its vibrancy, an amplifier for the needs of multilingual voices, and a point of departure for research into multilingual and transcultural writing.

I want to thank my very close team members and co-editors, who have dedicated a considerable part of their precious spare time to this book, for their commitment to words and dashes, and for all the laughs and worries we shared along the way — Filippo Bagnasco, Andrea Färber and Chiara Meitz; *Tinted Trails* guest editors and award-winning authors Marjorie Agosín and Juhea Kim for agreeing to the collaboration and for their encouraging support; prose editor Matthew Monroy and poetry editor John Salimbene for their invaluable opinions; art editor Vanesa Erjavec for her never-ending passion to create the most tinted cover, the best-fitting illustrations, and basically everything else art-wise; graphic designer Andreas Kolli for the many hours spent mulling over fonts, spacing, paper and line breaks; and the many writers and artists for agreeing to be published in this anthology and for connecting with Tint on many more levels. A complex undertaking such as an ESL anthology needs a widespread base of curious and eager minds, and I cannot thank all of them enough.

Leading a nonprofit organization dedicated to a niche, yet crucial and contemporary literary topic can be challenging. Thankfully, there are other organizations which support Tint's mission and vision, and many of them have agreed to also support the publication of *Tinted Trails* and collaborate with us in whatever possible way. Thus, thanks go to FORUM STADTPARK for publishing this book under the umbrella of their press, to the Afro-Asian Institute Graz for hosting our anniversary festivities, to *treffpunkt sprachen* at the University of Graz for supporting the production of the book to a considerable degree, and to the Center for Inter-American Studies at the University of Graz, uniT, The Pennyless Players, Radio Helsinki, *Megaphon* as well as Books4Life. Should any organization not be listed, I wish to point the readers to our website, www.tintjournal.com, where the spontaneity of the Internet allows for completion.

Of course, the financial aspect cannot be ignored when rolling out the involvement in *Tinted Trails*. Thus, I'd like to thank our project sponsors Land Steiermark Cultural Department, Stadt Graz Cultural Department and Mayor's Office, Alps-Adriatic Alliance and the University of Graz. A considerable role was also played by the supporters of our Kickstarter crowdfunding campaign: They set the tone for this endeavor by giving much more to the project than our initial goal had asked of them, and with their help, we could move *Tinted Trails* from the planning to the realization phase. All supporters are credited towards the end of the book.

Finally, kisses to everyone who gifted me with an open ear, an open mind, a well-wishing thought, a kind gesture, an inspiring quote, as well as reason and bravery throughout the many months that lead to this publication: my partner, my friends, my colleagues — thank you.

Now, dear reader, it is up to you. Your adventure through a translingual garden is ready to begin, the patches have been sown, watered and nourished, and the fruits are waiting for you to harvest them. Your journey through the texts will be self-guided, yet the organization into four thematic chapters — Belonging, (Im)migration, Upheaval and Identities — may serve as an aid for orientation, as do the content warnings that you find on the final pages. Should you wish to share your thoughts with me or my tinted team members, read more ESL texts, or listen to audio recordings of the authors reading their texts, please visit our website or send us an email. Literature does not have to be a one-way street; let us work together on refining this playground that holds such an immense plurality of meanings, chances and perspectives.

Tinted Trails is one of many steps into the vast landscape of translingual writing, and one contribution to the corpus of global literature in English. May many more follow.

Introduction
Marjorie Agosín

My childhood unfolded amid a variety of languages spoken by my family. At home everyone spoke Yiddish, but I also heard Russian from my paternal grandparents, German from my maternal grandparents, and I learned Hebrew at school. Although these foreign languages were distinct from the Spanish I spoke every day, their sounds and sweet melodies enriched my world and taught me to pay attention to the rhythms that each one produced. Over the years, I have come to believe that languages are not only gateways to different geographical territories but also offer us a unique glimpse into our souls.

I subconsciously began to write this essay in Spanish, fully knowing that *Tint Journal* is a magazine for authors who have chosen to write in English and not in their native language. This sudden realization made me wonder about the mysterious and almost magical properties of language, and why it is that people choose to express themselves in a language other than their own. It also compelled me to think more about what it means to write in a foreign tongue, and about the emotions that trigger the preference of one language over the other.

For many of the writers featured in *Tint Journal*, English becomes the language for speaking about home and about what was left behind. I often wonder if choosing a language other than one's own offers a certain respite and distance to alleviate the suffering experienced in exile. Does a writer intend to capture certain moments of the past to prepare for the present in a new language? Do they also think about the possibilities of a new language in a place of freedom where the imagination can be both boundless and restless?

Since I myself have experienced displacement, the subjects of forced migrations, authoritarianism, and exile are topics dear to my emotional memory and to my deepest of sentiments. I often have felt that my native tongue, Spanish, is closer to my creative life. However, I also communicate in English every day and feel comfortable both speaking and writing in my acquired second language.

I arrived in the United States during a pivotal time in my life. As a 15-year-old adolescent I was suddenly uprooted from my homeland and not only lost my sense of self but also my identity as a poet who wrote in Spanish. The first time I spoke English was when I was sent to high school in Athens, Georgia. And this compels me to wonder what it was like for the writers of *Tint Journal* when they first experienced the possibility of writing in English. Did they struggle with this new language, or did they quickly make it their own? *Tint Journal* offers a unique possibility to understand and to feel what it means to write in a foreign tongue. Moreover, it allows for both readers and writers to consider how acquired languages have the capacity to expand the possibility of a multilingual imagination.

A few years ago, when I first met Lisa Schantl in Graz, Austria, and later, when she invited me to collaborate on this anthology, I became fascinated by the vision and welcoming perspective that she and the editors of *Tint Journal* share. I was moved by their openness to welcome writers from all over the world who are concerned about issues of identity and displacement, as well as translingualism.

The poets and prose writers featured in this literary magazine are inquisitive in their abilities to pose questions and to reimagine their place in a world that can only become borderless through the power of their imagination. Not every writer in the magazine and this anthology shares the experience of forced displacement but I would say that they have all chosen to belong to a language that they have acquired by choice and that has enabled them to create a new identity that allows them to describe who they were before and who they are now.

Writing for so many creative artists is an exploration of identity that empowers them to develop a heightened awareness of themselves and of their place in the world. Those who have been forced into exile often try to capture a sense of belonging to a new and unfamiliar social and cultural context. I believe that Tint provides them with the opportunity to explore the unknown by nurturing a sense of freedom found in a newly acquired language.

Coming to the U.S. with no previous knowledge of English was an experience filled with cruelty. I was placed in a class where only English was spoken, and my schoolmates made fun of my accent. I felt culturally isolated from my classmates and my teacher, and since there was no ESL program in the educational system, the intensity of learning English was overwhelming. As a consequence, I struggled in my studies, and I did not feel welcomed in my newly adopted country.

Despite the fact that as a college professor I now teach courses in English and in expository writing, I still long for the sounds of Spanish, and I often wonder what would have happened to me if I had never left Chile and had continued writing in Spanish. Although the English language eventually became a part of my identity as a writer, I still only write poetry in Spanish because it is close to my memory of life before exile, and it is the language that taught me how to name my inner world.

All languages are bridges to unknown geographies that offer possibilities of becoming, and flowering again. I believe the authors in this special issue of Tint write about the way they have experienced their world, about what was left behind, and about their sense of identity and belonging. They all do it with grace and sophistication.

Tint is a refuge for writers, poets, and essayists alike. It is a space for the translingual imagination to both flourish and cultivate desire and creativity in a foreign tongue. The editors of *Tint Journal* respect this foreignness and accept diversity and inclusivity in times of polarization and racism. Julia Kristeva in her book *Strangers to Ourselves* speculates about the challenges and the losses of being a foreigner. The majority of the writers in this issue come from elsewhere and yet, they are motivated to find their new sites of memory in this journal that nurtures foreign voices.

As I think about this online literary magazine while having the honor to write these pages as a poetry guest editor, I contemplate the power of the translingual mind and what it means to write in two or more languages. Do we attempt to master them all, or do we remain satisfied with the imperfections of our newly acquired language? Steven Kellman, who wrote an important book called *The Translingual Imagination*, states that most translingual writers are emigrants. *Tint Journal* is a magazine that invites emigrant literature and welcomes individuals from diverse ethnicities. Perhaps this is why it is such an important and visionary platform for a time challenged by violence and social injustice. As a poet and human rights activist, I applaud this special magazine of Tint and as I write these words English also becomes a language of my choice.

Edited by Celeste Kostopulos-Cooperman

Introduction
Juhea Kim

When my family and I immigrated to the U.S. in 1996, I changed from a confident, bubbly child into one that hardly ever opened her mouth. At age 9, I didn't know the alphabet and had to start from scratch. Formerly a star student, I spent the entire day not understanding anything the teacher said. For over a year, I knew so little English that I sometimes arrived at an empty school after not getting that it was a holiday.

My utter incomprehension changed one day when I read *The Odyssey* in English. I still remember the paperback cover, the photo inset of Odysseus, Circe, Polyphemus, and other heroes, gods, and monsters. I was entranced by this world, and suddenly it didn't matter that I didn't understand half the words. I read underlining the unknown parts, but still falling in step with the narrative. It was the first time English felt like a key and not a wall.

From then on, reading and eventually creative writing in English became a way for me to claim space and assert myself. No one knows better than an immigrant the true power of language: Natural-born citizens wield it as evidence of their superiority; those who acquired it as a second language are asked to doubt themselves constantly. Job applications require people to check off "native," "fluent," or "proficient" next to their languages, and no matter how I feel about English, I would have to say I'm only "fluent" in it because it is my second language.

Recently, I went to a party where I met a wealthy white couple who were neighbors with my friend, D. When I said D was mischievous, the husband and wife looked back at me confused until the wife exclaimed, "Oh, you mean mis-CHI-VI-ous." The husband nodded like he finally understood a word that I'd mispronounced. And I, an Ivy-educated author (who writes in

English!), came home and checked the online dictionary to make sure I'd been right, instead of correcting the couple on the spot on their mistake.

The truth is that learning English as a second language (ESL) is something that affects you far beyond the first few confusing years. It has lifelong consequences, whether one chooses to seriously pursue creative writing or simply carries on living in an English-dominated world. But despite all the annoyances and real prejudices I've experienced, I still wouldn't trade the gift of being multilingual. The simultaneous access to my mother tongue (Korean), my second language (English), and my third language (French) has enriched my life and unlocked my creativity in ways that otherwise would have been impossible. This is because your language shapes your values, and your values shape your art. Without my linguistic background, I wouldn't have become the artist that I am today.

Nevertheless, being an ESL person adds an invisible layer of penalty in an increasingly English-dominated world. This is especially true in the field of literature and publishing, where not only English grammar but even its particular aesthetic preferences continue to reign. The condemnation of adverbs, or any alternative words to "say," or the favoring of long sentences all point to English hegemony. Just a little healthy exposure to world literature debunks these "rules" as absolute: The Russian masterpieces are filled with adverbs, and East Asian writing shows a different kind of elegance afforded by a short sentence structure.

Unfortunately, current publishing standards penalize writers who are less likely to conform to these English "rules." This is a loss to both talented writers and the publishing world, which can benefit from opening its doors to new ideas, values, aesthetics, and languages.

This is why *Tint Journal*'s mission to publish ESL writers is so urgently needed. Let it be said that writing is art, and publishing is business. But literary magazines stand somewhere in-between. Just as no (true) writer goes into writing to make money or become famous, a literary magazine isn't founded to earn any type of financial or worldly profit. On the contrary, it's likely to cost its founders, editors, and readers a great deal of trouble over many years if the journal is successful. But no other platform exists to nurture a young writer the way a literary magazine does. Before I'd published a book, I had published short stories with several literary magazines that made me feel like I was on the right path. It was validating, encouraging, and nurturing in a crucial — even life-changing — way.

Tint fills the gap in this ecosystem, where ESL writers — many of whom are ethnically or socioeconomically underrepresented — are invited to speak in their own voice. Tint allows them to write in English, the lingua franca without which serious literary success is even harder; but it also acknowledges and highlights the native and other languages that inform them. This openness, fraternity, acceptance and celebration of our human diversity are what publishing needs to deliver art and stories that matter — and indeed, it is what the world needs now more than ever.

Μ. Καραγεώργιου

BELONGING

Belonging is a process. We might perceive it as a fixed state, because once we truly belong it seems that we have already arrived at our intended destination, but in truth it is "a process that is fuelled by yearning rather than the positioning of identity as a stable state."[7] Belonging is also, thus, a choice. We cannot decide where we are born, who we are born as, or the ties that connect us to our ancestry. But we can choose where, what, or whom we belong with. By making these conscious decisions, we open ourselves up to enter into relationships with those places, spaces, and beings that we want to engage with. I think that it is important here to differentiate between "belonging to" and "belonging with." To "belong to," for me, implies a power imbalance that erases the aspect of free will. To "belong with," on the other hand, allows for a conscious decision of aligning our lives with those things that matter most to us. I belong with my loved ones and I belong with literature, just to give an example, because these are two of the things that make me the happiest. Both of them require effort, time, and commitment, like everything does that we aspire to be a part of.

When we want to belong, it always involves the aspect of desire; after all, belonging always includes longing. We long to become part of something bigger. Belonging is not a goal. Rather, it is a never-ending journey on a path that twists and turns. Without effort, we can only dream of walking that path. While we are on that journey towards belonging, we might encounter junctions and recognize that the way we are headed no longer reflects who we want to be. It takes bravery to make the choice to branch off from our current trail, but if we long for something else, we can only find fulfillment and happiness by following our ever-changing desires.

The texts in this section reflect this journey to find spaces in societies, cultures, relations, and physical places. They grapple with social relationships and family ("The Liars' Village"), with language ("Amphibian"), war ("My Azov Sea"), and heritage ("The Brother Moves On"). These authors, in their fiction, poetry, and nonfiction texts, ask us, their characters, and themselves, what it means to belong both "to" and "with." How can we navigate the spaces that we belong to without being given a choice, and how can we connect with the ones we truly want to belong with? The ESL authors in this anthology have all made the decision that their texts belong with the English language for various reasons, allowing us as readers a glimpse into their own vulnerable paths towards belonging by expressing their thoughts and feelings in their non-native language.

by Andrea Färber

Amphibian
Natalie Bühler

Poetry

NATIONALITY Swiss
FIRST LANGUAGE Swiss German
SECOND LANGUAGES English & French

Appeared in Issue Spring '22

Slide in for a bilingual swim, brain suddenly porous,
Grammar shifts but lexicon remains, the sun casts
The same net on the pool floor,
Pebbles petrified in concrete
And that beating breath
Then, movement
Pushing with my frog legs
To run a zipper-line across the surface:

One, two — HAH
    Eis, zwoi — HAH
        Du bisch denn en wasserratte

                I floated in unsalted pools then, watching the frogs
                    Migrate at dawn, goosebumped arms
                        Sticking out of wet swimmers
                            Turn — HAH
                        Push off the wall — HAH
                  Lingered until fingertips were shrivelling;
            What a funny expression away from home, a water-rat

        Eis, two, wait —
    Which language do I count in
Swallow saline — HAH

Remember to swim on the left — remember the pool
In Winterthur, so welcoming on lonely afternoons
Don't think of distance, don't sink
800, *800*, just fifty left — HAH
Crawl back, *eis, zwoi* — HAH
Can't remember my mother's rash
After decades of working in chlorine;
Just that frog's skin is so porous it'll poison them
So we'd fish out and walk them to their home in the pond

One, two, HAH
    Bubbles drowning noise — pull up into air again
        Mami, ich bin hüt ändlich wider go schwümme
        And walk myself home as far as I can.

The Liars' Village
Lindi Dedek

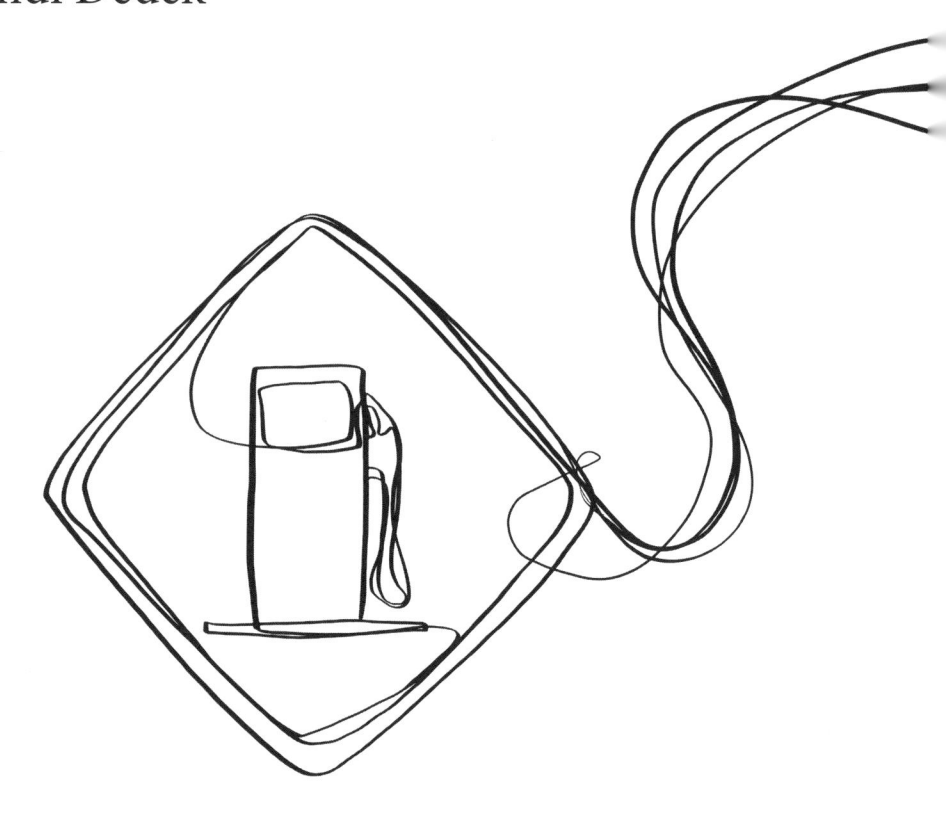

Fiction

NATIONALITY Czech
FIRST LANGUAGE Czech
SECOND LANGUAGES English, German, French & Spanish

Appeared in Issue Fall '22

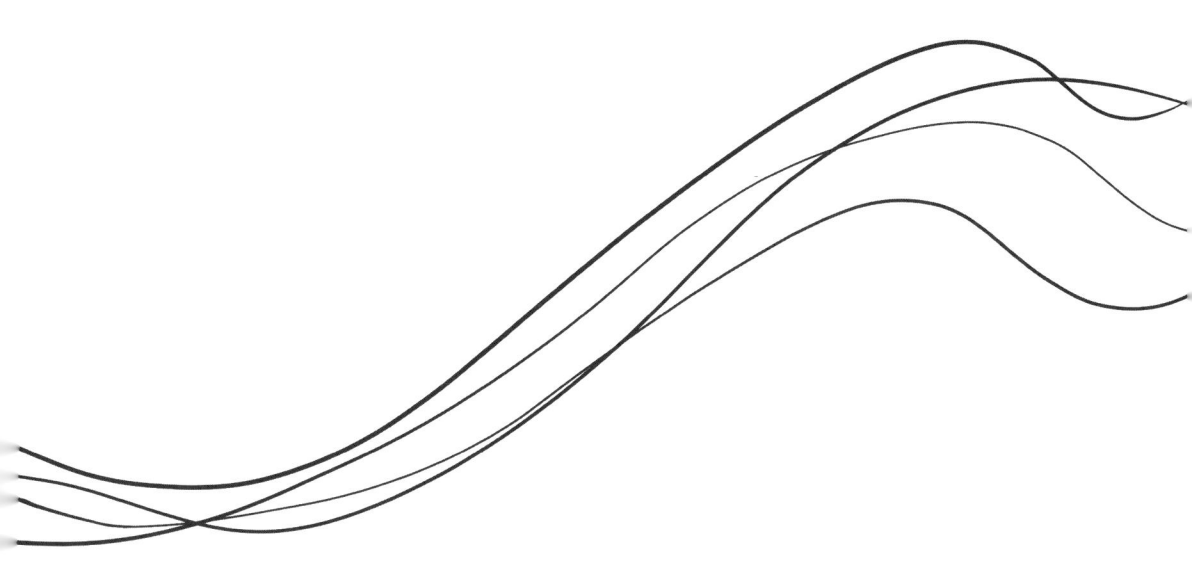

The gas station marks our weekly trips. It splits the time into quarters. When we stop there on Saturday morning, we'll need exactly three quarters of an hour to get to my grandma's house.

These mornings are filled with the pursuit of that weekend fantasy land, with grandma's grilled chicken, peach fruit stew and mashed potatoes. Unlimited TV time and VHS in the winter; garden playtime in the summer. It doesn't take much to persuade dad to drive me to grandma's every weekend.

When we leave our ugly town behind, with its factory chimneys and polluted Elbe, villages and villages emerge after every hill, one more boring than the next till we reach Lzovice, translated as the Liars' Village, name origin unknown. It is where our weekend landmark stands.

The gas station is situated on a country road in the middle of nowhere in central Bohemia, too far from anything significant to give you a point of reference, it's the middle of the middle of nowhere.

For Lzovice and the nearby villages, the gas station serves many functions after the corner store and the pub closed down following the revolution. It's a cross-generational gathering club, a bar, and a grocery store for those in-between town trips, and an ice cream parlor. Bearing little resemblance to any of the anonymous Shells, Arals or ESSOs that started to pop up like mushrooms in the recent years on the newly built highways, this gas station is a proud enterprise of a local family. It was established in 1990, after the Iron Curtain fell and the country opened for new business.

We stop and I ask my dad how far it is. A gentle move on my side, as this is a question I know he knows the answer to. I stopped bothering to engage with him a while ago. I must have been about 3 years old when I found out that he wasn't generous in his attention. On one of the rare occasions when mum assigned him with childcare, the two of us once played a memory game in the living room of our first flat. We were sitting on the scratchy, dark red Persian carpet. His melancholic look drifted from the little cartoon playing cards, designed by the Czech Bank to help kids learn English. Despite my encouraging hints as to which card he needed to turn so the Czech sun could shine alongside the English one and the red Czech and English bike could ride together, he just couldn't care less. My obvious victory at the end of the game only left me annoyed.

The gas station Plihal & Plihalova is nothing more than a plain white cubicle with a glass front and four gas stands under a metal roof, with a surprising variety of stock. Cans of peas, pears and pasta slowly approach their expiration date. The gossip newspaper screams the headlines behind the shiny, overpriced Swiss chocolates. Crappy toys also approach an expiration date of a week after purchase. Last time I got a shiny turning wheel toy that broke down before we reached grandma's house.

The station's interior decoration consists of a microwave where you can heat up wiener sausages, with the mustard standing right next to the bread basket. Carefully arranged plants, mostly sansevierias, called mother-in-laws' tongues in Czech, have their sharp tongues sticking out in all directions. Plihalova waters the tongues every other day. She's a tall middle-aged woman with the unmistakably 90s mahogany hair color. Her husband Plihal is a large man in his late forties. His chestnut curls move further away from his forehead every time we see him. The couple is always up for a good chat with their customers, especially when served with a glass of wine. The Plihals curate an astonishing selection of wine for this area and era.

I realized some time ago that dad would buy me anything in the world or at least at the gas station, and I usually choose ice cream. I adore the prickly, cactus-shaped one. I open my mouth wide and let it dissolve on my tongue for more of the sparkling effect, watching my dad and Plihal talking and drinking sparkling wine. Just five more minutes, dad's soft voice promises, and Plihalova pats my head and nods. Sometimes she hands me a lollipop or a second ice cream cone.

When dad's in a good mood, he adds a newspaper for grandma. The relationship between him and his in-laws is getting more constricted with the success of his security camera business.

When we arrive at her house way past noontime, she's done reading the paper and tends to her garden (after her retirement, grandma built a pond with waterlilies in her garden and reads German papers in the mornings). Grandma shouts coffee! coffee! at dad as if she was a pizzeria server but he waves her offer off with the antenna of his new cellphone and drives away, I presume back to the gas station.

The gas station is where we get the guilt-plagued box of chocolate for my mum when my dad picks me up two hours too late again. My mum adores perfumes, makeup and fashion. No matter what she does, her makeup is intact and matches the color of her clothes and the new trends from *Harper's Bazaar* or *Elle*. She came a long way from having only that one red lipstick per year smuggled from Western Germany. She doesn't need to press the color out till the last bit and break her lip over the sharp edge.

Her impressive display of scents and makeup boxes looks stunning on the marble shelves in the bathroom in our new house, each item telling us how often my father slipped or disappeared. My mum is excellent at painting happiness over her sad, resigned face. I love watching her precise remake ritual before she enters her dentist practice in the morning and the equally ceremonial facial removal in the evening.

The gas station is also where I get my gray-striped plush cat. My parents remain resistant to my wish of a real pet so they let me have a stuffed dummy as a practice tool for kindness and care cultivation. I call the cat Liki, a fusion of my name and Japanese anime. I make her a hand-drawn birth certificate and for about three months Liki is a living animal to me until I start school, and can't take care of her any longer.

During the 90s, my parents and I become devoted students of the significance of gifts. We study their delicate powers of speaking to other humans — heart-to-heart — like no one else can. Their ability to communicate affection, attention, abuse; over the years establishing a special Morse code, that's not special at all: working late / flowers. Lashing out during lunch time / praline box. Getting carried away by someone's cleavage during your company summer party / taking your daughter to an aquapark. Not coming home from your company summer party / Dior's new perfume release.

Ten years later, it's the gas station where my best friend Jolanka and I have our first job, as window cleaners. We need to offer to clean the window shields of every driver who passes Lzovice.

Dad organized it. He says it pays well, even when only in tips, which we confirm to him when he picks us up after the first shift. He lives in a world of fixed gender roles and conservative manners, so he informs us that with our first earnings we're supposed to buy presents for our parents. Jolanka and I have never heard of that tradition before, but we've also never had a job before. He chooses two Raffaello packages in the station shop and two identical bouquets of gerbera daisies, and pays for them. We give them to our moms.

The rest of the summer of the window cleaning job feels like the rest of the summer in our town: dull with an occasional thrill. Some days, we score high bank notes without having to clean the car windows. On other days, we beat our day earning record, or the tequila shots drinking record at a death metal festival in the village behind Lzovice. The fast cash dissolves any prejudice we might have held against this job.

One morning it starts pouring, just half an hour after Jolanka and I arrived at the gas station. We can't decide if we want to raincheck the shift or wish the rain away, when a mountain biker emerges behind a hill. A short brown ponytail sticks out from under the helmet, a white shirt, baggy beige trousers. She looks about ten years older than us. She descends from her bike, and approaches us to ask in English about an accommodation nearby.

We sit down together at the wooden tables under the roof. She raises her eyebrows when we tell her about our job. Her eyes show amusement and concern at the same time. She's so different from Plihal's usual guests. Plihal and a small group of regulars come out of the shop and gather around us.

Jolanka and I become the translators between Lzovice and the world. We're not sure if we're more surprised that she's biking alone around the world or that she decided to stop at this gas station of all places. And how the hell did she get on a bike from Australia — she took a plane to China, she admits. She gives us her email address, globetrotter[at]something.australia, and leaves again, and I'd like to say that the sun comes out again but it doesn't.

Plihalova lets me paraphrase the conversation again and again. I glow with the possibility of adventures unthinkable an hour ago. What a dyke,

Plihalova notes at one point. I ask how she picked this up, the biker didn't mention any partner. Exactly, her husband says. The local crowd laughs and Jolanka whispers let's go, the next train comes in 40 minutes. We hide in the corner and buy lemon tea from the drinks machine with our train money.

Jolanka's dad, a journalist in a local radio and my drama teacher, chases the Australian biker for an interview the next day, but she's long gone.

A couple of days later on a rainy day, I'm walking around town, my steps following the disoriented orders of my teenage head: I know neither where to go, nor what to think. I pass Jolanka's house but she's not in and Jolanka's dad insists on giving me a ride. He says he has to go somewhere, his destination as vague as mine.

In his car, he plays an *Easy English* tape, an unusual choice of tune. As we're driving through town, I wonder if it'd be faster to walk. He keeps talking, he keeps shouting; I can't quite follow his stories. I ask myself if the beer bottles under my seat have something to do with his voice.

At one point he says my dad should take care of himself and I wonder what sort of question is that. Then he stops the car in front of the old men pub, much older men pub, the white hair or bald men pub, on the main street across from my parents' house. I leave the car and my confusion leaves the car with me.

I call my dad and when he doesn't pick up, I try the gas station. He's coming home soon, Plihal tells me, but he isn't. I hide behind my rooftop room window and observe the calm street.

When I see Jolanka's dad finally leaving the pub, his legs spin into each other like a pretzel, his arms twist around someone's neck. And that someone is my mother.

The affair leaks out in a telenovela fashion the first week of school. Jolanka and I are at the drama club and act in Genet's *Maids* under the direction of her dad. After the performance, Jolanka's mum comes to my mum and crosses her arms. She points to Jolanka and her husband and says, This is my husband. This is my family. I want you to see us this way. Where's your husband? I will make sure he comes next time if you don't.

My mum looks right through her and we leave. I propose we pick dad up at the gas station but mum can't drive through her tears.

Later Jolanka accuses me of asking her dad to drive me home and then disappearing for two days. As if it was my mistake that we live close to the pub. As if it was my mistake that it turns out he had a year-long affair with my mum.

Jolanka sits away from me the first week of school. Since then, I've been working at the gas station alone, on September weekends before the weather gets too bad.

One day someone pulls over in an 80s gray Mercedes. The driver has an intense, alien glow in his asphalt eyes and says he's 19, but he looks like he's 30. He doesn't want me to clean his windows, but he buys me an ice cream. Don't worry I'm clean, he says and hands me a cigarette. He wants to know when my shift ends. I say that I'm my own boss but I need the cash. He says he'll pick me up in an hour. I'm frightened and repulsed, so I say yes.

When he returns to the gas station 59 minutes later, Plihal takes me aside and imposes that I can't drive home with a drug addict, and sends him away. I hear my loud voice telling him that everyone in Lzovice is drunk-driving and that this guy has been clean for months, to which Plihal responds that it's bullshit, which he might be right about. I don't want to deal with Plihal anymore so I call it a day. I walk to the train station and the Mercedes pulls off.

In the car we listen to dubstep. I tell Glow that I'm tired of being 16 because I can't vote or drive or run away to Australia. He says he doesn't understand my worries and parks in front of the socialist building of the Orion club, the crystal meth mecca. Before disappearing inside, Glow asks me if I wanted to try something special today. I say I'll think about it. Glow keeps calling me the whole summer, but I never answer.

After the weekend, Srkal says that the gas station shifts are taken till the end of the year. The word of mouth reaches my parents that it's because of my sharp tongue, lack of respect to elders and dubious friendships. I'm tired of proving them wrong.

Several weeks later, word of mouth spills from Lzovice again — my father was stopped drunk-driving right after the hill behind the gas station on his way home. His driver's license is gone, maybe for good. Apparently he's been buying Bohemia Sekt brut at the gas station every fucking night of the last ten years, Plihal and him sharing a bottle, sometimes two.

Dad was furious for nine months until he got his license back. He spends more time at home, which makes mum file for divorce. He's convinced he was spied on, going through the possible culprits. It's interesting but not surprising that he only blames men. Mum and I look down when he asks who we think it was. As nobody goes to the gas station, we are left without our supplies of chocolate, so we only have our nails to bite into when he interrogates us.

Despite Jolanka's mum's intervention, some secrets remain uncovered and some marriages flourish, which makes Jolanka finally come around. Jolanka confesses to me over a bottle of cheap champagne that we nicked from dad, that her mum forgave my mum for the sake of our friendship. I think it might be in exchange of my mum letting Jolanka stay with us. Her parents go on a month-long vacation to Croatia, for the first time since their honeymoon, as Jolanka's mum doesn't forget to emphasize.

Soon it will be summer again and we will need to look for summer jobs. Reluctantly, the gas station crosses our mind. As it turns out, it's the gas station's last year in business and a bad one. The Plihals won't be able to keep up with the gas prices, and the gas station with their health. Plihal will be diagnosed with a brain tumor, and then a few days later Plihalova will fall ill with lung cancer. They recover but the gas station will be transformed into a Shell.

Grandma will find us a job in the fish factory in her town, changing the oil stink and heated asphalt for mackerel and roes, making the summer wet and cold.

My Azov Sea
Viktoriia Grivina

Nonfiction

NATIONALITY   Ukrainian
FIRST LANGUAGE   Ukrainian
SECOND LANGUAGE   English

Appeared in Issue Fall '22

In the early autumn of 2021, I repeated my old childhood route from Kharkiv to the sea of Azov. There, in the lazy silence of Schastlivtsevo (The Lucky Village) as the holiday season was rolling to its close, I felt a tremendous moment of quiet before the storm.

The September sea along the thin land strip of the Arabat Spit was quiet and cold. My friend and I came on a bus at dawn, and, surrounded by a pack of stray and strangely menacing huskies (the most bizarre Stephen Kingian sort of danger I'd ever experienced), walked to the white ribbon of the beach. The Spit with its longest, but not necessarily cleanest, beach in Europe is covered in crushed shells — rakushnyak. Rakushnyak is ever present. Houses are built with it, and the ground is made of it, and my hair and lungs instantly filled with it too. The Spit stretches all the way to Crimea. In 2014, Russians, exercising the privilege of force and terror over the international community, occupied not only Crimea but half of the Spit too. An elderly couple on the bus on our way here had asked the driver if they would be able to cross to "the Russian side." The driver looked at them with a quiet understanding gaze of a psychiatrist dealing with a curious case, and agreed to drop the couple off at the last village on the Spit. An additional payment of 50 hryvnias was duly paid.

The Arabat Spit also known as Strelka ("arrow") cuts the Azov sea from Syvash, a chain of shallow lagoons, filled with salt and all kinds of marine life: small bychki fishes ("little bulls," bony fish), iglas ("needles," pipefish) and tiny local shrimps, good enough when boiled with dill and a herb called soleros (salicornia). Everything is not what it seems: Bychki are not bulls, iglas aren't needles, and the shrimps are nothing like those in a supermarket. Soleros is the only thing that is what it is. "Sol" means salt, and "ros" to grow. Like the crushed shells, soleros grows everywhere from Azov to the salty meadows of Syvash. You can taste it at a local restaurant of high cuisine, with balsamic vinegar and German Riesling. Or pick for free on the beach after swimming in the shallow Azov, then add to your tomato salad.

Growing up I spent every summer here with my grandpa who was rewarded by the Komsomolsk power plant with a seasonal managerial position at the plant's holiday house. No one in our family knew what grandpa did as an employee of the power plant for the rest of the year, since the only qualification we knew he had was as a teacher of arts and crafts. Such were Ukrainian 1990s, filled with wonder and salary payments in the form of Earl Grey tea that grandpa once extracted from the plant, making my dad drink it for a year despite my dad's inborn dislike of bergamot.

The road from Kharkiv was a ten-hour adventure wrapped in boiling heat, smell of corn, freshwater crabs and chebureki (fried thin Tatar pies with meat), which every passenger felt the urge to buy on those roadside markets you could recognize from afar by beach towels swaying in the wind. A tiger, a naked lady and a dollar sign were the three most popular patterns on the towels. On the road back somewhere around Novomoskovsk, well-rested workers of the power plant would also buy sets of painted enamel bowls, courtesy of the local enamel factory workers and their businesses on the side. Because grandpa always shook hands with the right people I could enjoy this adventure for free. In Komsomolsk my mom would put me on an overturned crate next to the driver, and on Azov grandpa would be waiting with a gigantic Kherson watermelon, to buy me out. I felt like one of those Cossacks who got captured and returned from the Istanbul slave traders after their families had paid the arranged price.

My wild summer would start then and there, melting in the sweet syrup of melons and peaches, the buzz of mosquitoes and the ever-lasting boredom of Azov. Unlike Crimea, which had always been too expensive for an honest family like ours, the Spit did not have much to offer to a wandering eye. It was just an endless beach with a lonely tree by the road, a herd of cows and an occasional farmer's plane — kukuruznik — that sprinkled sunbathers with mosquito poison. To my dad it was perfect. The most he'd spend would be a couple of hryvnias for my paprika crisps and strawberry Cornetto ice cream.

We'd waste time playing blackjack on the beach, using shells for money, and catching shrimps on Syvash with the lace curtain we'd take off the window in grandpa's hotel room. Once a week we'd go "to the city" of Henichesk, and buy a huge meaty pelengas fish (redlip mullet), to cook it on a barbecue with herbs and baby potatoes. And every evening I'd watch (for free, the courtesy of grandpa's connections) the two films our hotel cinema had — *Lion King* and *Ace Ventura*. I knew them by heart.

My dad would sometimes drive from work for a weekend and take us to Crimea in his old white Soviet car. We'd go through the Spit and all along the southern coast to Yalta and Alupka's Vorontsov palace. I could hardly believe my eyes thinking that these mountains and beaches were "mine." During my teenage years my rebellion was to abandon Azov for Crimea and hike with Kharkiv Polytechnic tourist club, sleeping in tents at the wild beaches, drinking sweet Massandra wine and jumping into the deep Black Sea from the rocks. Another impossible thing for the shallow shores of Azov.

I never got to visit the main Crimean festivals, the notorious KaZantip, or a more cultured Koktebel Jazz. It felt like something you could always do later. Like Donetsk or Luhansk. After 2014, Koktebel Jazz lost its home base of, well, Koktebel, and became a nomadic on- and off-event. And now in 2021 it was advertised as the last music happening of the holiday season.

My friend, who had been to the real Koktebel Jazz, was disillusioned already when we jumped off the bus. The first thing she noted, there was no music coming from anywhere. Everything but the wild husky pack seemed to sleep. We walked through the wind, squinting at the rising sun, and called our Airbnb host. A tall quiet woman in a beige headscarf greeted us by the tall gates. She didn't mind us arriving five hours earlier, as we seemed to be the only tourists around. Having shown us the room, she walked off to the beach with her kids. I didn't need to ask to know our hosts were Crimean Tatars. It wasn't just about the headscarf. Only those who've lost a sea once can appreciate it.

Back in Crimea — when it was still mine before 2014 — I once stayed at a former Tatar house too. My host was an old Russian woman whose husband had worked in a mine in Donbas and received the house as a thank you from the Soviet government. After 1944 the peninsula was subjected to massive resettlement, where you mostly had to be ethnically Russian to have the right to move in. Ukrainians weren't welcome, though also not persecuted for visiting. Unlike Krymchaks (one of the names of Crimean Tatars) who were banned from the peninsula until 1989. The house was situated straight on the territory of the national park, and I stayed in a wing, built apparently for the household animals, but still sturdy enough. The well in the garden was dry — not many Russian settlers knew how to take care of natural springs as they would often come from very different landscapes, therefore the situation with water in Crimea had been slowly deteriorating since the 1940s. I would always get "the second-day food poisoning," a reward for forgetting to not cook with water from the tap. When asked, my elderly host preferred to keep silent about the original owners of the house. Soviet people, taught by the system, never liked Krymchaks. I often wondered afterwards, if, like many, she'd met the descendants of the owners, if they ever knocked at her door in the 1990s, showing old photographs, asking to look around. Soviet settlers tended to treat Tatars with aggression coming, very understandably, from guilt.

In Schastlivtsevo our host's house, pool and a chain of motel-like rooms were clean and freshly painted. Only poisonous spiders that we brought in the bouquets of wildflowers would sometimes pop up on my bed, making me scream in surprise.

Koktebel Jazz was a pale shadow of its normal self, my friend would admit. The holiday season over, trucks with ice cream and cold beer were shutting down, and the evening shows on the beach featured three moderately drunk men in their 50s feeding cats on an empty dance floor by the stage. Algae, wind and seagulls were taking over the vast emptiness for the winter. On the second day of the festival we walked to the Pink Lake instead. A family looking for the lake picked us up, even though we didn't hitchhike specifically. "We all here need to help each other," the father in the driver's seat said. He used to spend summers in Crimea as a child. Now Azov became the main place for his three kids.

Driving back from the Spit a day later, I looked at the Syvash lagoon, trying to imagine how salt merchants of the 18th century — chumaks — dried salt along the coast, and took dangerous summer rides through the wild steppes teaming with nomadic criminal squadrons, to sell salt and bring prosperity to their villages. There's a town called Valky in my region — named after a cart filled with chumak salt.

I was coming back to Kharkiv with bouquets of soleros instead. Azov was quiet, sleepy, ready for the winter, as if my last look at its waters sealed it for the next time. But also, somehow, the atmosphere was alert, somehow irrationally nervous. The feeling that half of the Spit was occupied, and that there, after a certain line we used to drive through every summer, now Russian soldiers stood their guard, brought ominous thoughts. As if I could hear those soldiers speak between one another in the distance. I lay sleepless during the nights, listening to the dark.

A friend who was driving from the Black Sea picked us up in Melitopol on the way back. Like mine, her stories were both cheerful — a surfing weekend — and sad — stories of persecuted Crimeans she was working with. We stopped by the museum of Melitopol, a beautiful 1913 mansion hidden behind white poplars. We walked around the garden and the collection of Scythian gold. Our guide said they'd won the Ukrainian Cultural Fund Grant and were expecting the restoration to begin. The gold is now looted and — like in ancient times — taken to the centre of the empire, with the director Leila Ibragimova kidnapped. I don't know if it has to do with Leila being Crimean. But I'm grateful that I saw this island of southern Ukrainian culture before, even if I know I'll see it again.

It was a strange feeling of hope and silence when we returned to the highway. I did not want to abandon it. As if, leaving, we were calling for winter to come. A sign showed the Stone Grave national reserve on the right. Our friend said she had always wanted to have a look. Why not, we answered, and drove into the hot steppes of Zaporizhia. The Stone Grave is a natural arrangement of large stones used for thousands of years by a variety of tribes for rituals and other unknown purposes. The natural reserve is a sandy terrain, and many Scythian and Polovets idols, called Babas, have been brought here from the surrounding ancient burial sites — kurgans. Kurgans pop up in the steppes from the Black Sea all the way to Kharkiv. Ukrainian warrior Cossacks considered them the graves of their ancestors and stopped to pray to the Babas. Today these idols are under protection of the government. Walking along the Stone Grave I felt like an actor in the *Star Wars* movies, it was a space-like kind of landscape. Tiny vipers skirted gravel paths under my feet. But I wasn't scared. There are places where rationale halts.

There are such times too. I had dreamt of the Stone Grave for a week before the new Russian invasion began. In my dreams I walked between the stones, and the sea of Azov, like an overturned mirror, looked at me from above.

In February the Russian army occupied the Spit, bizarrely erecting the statue of Lenin in Henichesk. The last thing I heard about Schastlivtsevo village was that someone tore the Russian flag off the village council and put the Ukrainian back. The news was shared by the Crimean Tatar Facebook community.

Every day the war was stepping closer — I read about the ancient Stone Grave in the news in March, a missile fell into the debris of the sandy ground. The lands around the Grave have now been covered in Russian mines. Melitopol museum was looted and bombed.

The war stepped closer — to my home region of Kharkiv, which I returned to on that late and hot September evening. The war came to the stone Babas on the mount Kremenets, their empty eyes overlooking the town of Izium down in the valley. The house of my cousin's aunt stands there as silent as the emptiness we hear in the receiver when trying to dial familiar numbers — we haven't heard from them since March 2.

The war came closer to my home city of Kharkiv — to the old Ukrainian fortress of Chuguiv, the home of "a famous Russian painter" Ilya Repin, who was born into an old Cossack family and grew up painting churches along the tall grassy banks of Donets river. On February 24, one of the first Russian missiles hit the Aviator district, and my other cousins threw their children in the car and drove through the night filled with sirens and fire, never looking back.

The war came closer — to the "East Village" (Vostochny) in the outskirts of Kharkiv to the house where I grew up, when my parents called and, trying not to sound alarming, mentioned a missile that landed on the driveway behind their car, and the chipped glass from the nearby windows littering the fresh layer of the recently renovated tarmac.

It then broke into central Kharkiv, to the crossroads of Science Avenue and Culture street, the street on which the Ukrainian writers' house was shelled. A couple of streets from where I'd been dropped off in the early September of 2021, with a bouquet of soleros and an enormous Kherson watermelon in a tote bag. The war came to the apartment I'd walked into after my trip to Azov. The apartment where that warm September night we ate the watermelon with prosecco, and where the bouquet of soleros still hangs from a nail on a balcony. Volunteers were living there, and now it is empty, as my friends and I are trying to assemble our lives elsewhere, in hope we would return.

The war came into my body on February 24, when I started trembling and never stopped, and still, sometimes, I shake suddenly, and objects fall out of my hands. I sit on the floor and let myself shake every once in a while, like a stalk of soleros, waiting for the land to stabilize. It happens when Kharkiv is being shelled, and my dad won't answer the phone. I wake up from explosions in my dreams, or a message of another bombed museum. I wake up and try to find the news about Henichesk, the occupied Arabat Spit, about Krymchaks. It's not a flashy topic. I now return to Azov in my mind, and miss its beautiful boredom. Among the fears of its extinction, the mines and soleros disappearing, I want to know there is a place that looks exactly like it did yesterday when my grandpa bought me out with a Kherson watermelon.

Still Life with Deer
Wil-Lian Guzmanos

Nonfiction

NATIONALITY   Filipino & Taiwanese
FIRST LANGUAGE   Filipino
SECOND LANGUAGES   English, Fukien & Mandarin Chinese

Appeared in Issue Spring '22

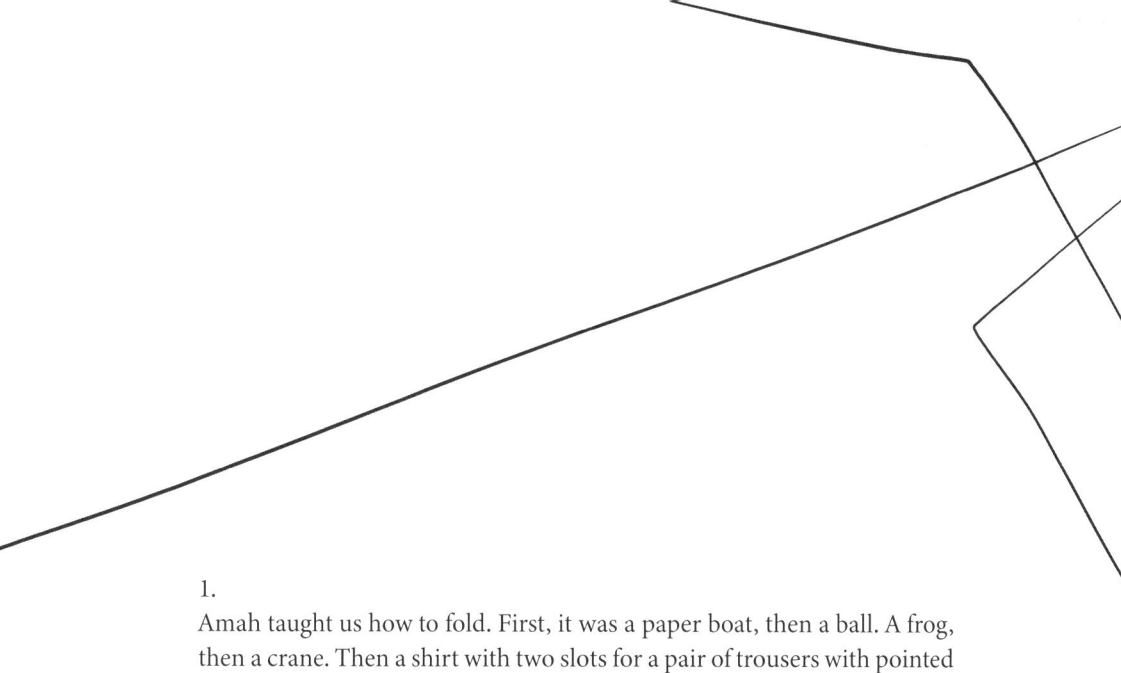

1.
Amah taught us how to fold. First, it was a paper boat, then a ball. A frog, then a crane. Then a shirt with two slots for a pair of trousers with pointed hems. When we ran out of glue, we used sticky rice to fold fans. The most beautiful thing she had ever made was a woven deer. She would undo the strips of her worn-out abanico fan and choose the ones with the right length. When she passed away, I asked Saku, my third uncle, if I could have the woven deer. He shook his head and kept it, together with the turquoise Underwood typewriter and the coal stove, which my cousin now uses during cookouts. Good thing he didn't give the deer to me. Otherwise, I would've unravelled it to find out how to make it. In my uncle's studio, the deer now lies in one of his old Japanese chest drawers.

2.
In the days following Amah's death, my four uncles and my aunt sorted through her closet, drawers, and cabinets for things they could keep and throw away. My grandmother had always been a private and reticent person, prone to angry outbursts whenever her things went missing. Had she been alive and well, she would have been outraged seeing them go through her clothes, jewelry, bags, and cans of Danish cookies, where she had kept her buttons and threads. I remember my youngest uncle, Kuku, securing a box with packing tape, which screeched relentlessly as he ripped it off its roll. What happened to the bottles of unused Green Cross alcohol, the one that Amah applied on her skin to keep herself cool on hot summer days? Where were her cereal bowl, spoon, mug, and plates? Who used them after we had left? Did they know they used to belong to someone who's now dead? Her clothes were either donated or burnt during the burial to provide for her in the afterlife. My aunt and my mother got hold

of her jewelry and knitwork. Who got to finish the Nescafé Classic instant coffee she would always have in the morning without milk? Or the Danish cookies in the blue round tin can? Where's the jar of brown sugar I stole spoonfuls of as a child? Who got to keep her Bicycle playing cards? Where did the stacks of *United Daily News* Amah used to read with a magnifying glass go? Did she leave anything behind for me?

3.
Saku once told me that when the Japanese forces reached Amoy, China, where Amah spent her youth, she saw a soldier run after her friend in the fields with a bayonet. She never saw her friend again. Whenever the soldiers came, she disguised herself as a man and hid inside the closet. They said she was starting to lose her mind so my great grandparents decided to escape to Manila with her.

4.
Amah lived her whole life in fear. The war destroyed her notion of time. The past just never seemed to come to a halt. She believed that an external force greater than her was trying to hurt her. Towards the end of her life, she saw silhouettes outside the window; hence, the closed blinds. She heard the people on television calling her name. She saw people in restaurants staring at her. In her youth, she would lock herself in her room whenever there were visitors. Days after the burial, I was sitting on the double glider in the living room and found her maintenance pills in one of the cushions. She fervently believed that doctors were trying to poison her.

5.
Siku, my fourth uncle, walked out of Amah's bedroom. He ruffled my hair when he saw me. He would only do that to Billy, his giant black Labrador, whose fur shines in the sun. Siku stepped out of the house to the garage and, through the screen door, I saw him take his glasses off and wipe his puffy face with a handkerchief. When all of them had finally left, I opened Amah's bedroom door. Her things were not in the places where they used to be. The familiar smell of Green Cross alcohol, Johnson's baby powder, and Ivory soap had somehow left the room, too. The air was heavy and the silence was deafening. Had she been alive, a slight alteration would have escalated to yelling and accusations and, as an admittance of mistake,

concluded in a blaring quietness when the object of interest was found. Enmeshed in that same stillness in her room, now even more deafening, I realized that she was indeed gone — Amah wouldn't have left her blinds open, more so let other people touch them. She wouldn't have let her closet be stripped bare of her things. She wouldn't have let the pictures of herself standing next to a Christmas tree in Rockwell or locked in an embrace with her daughter during her stay in L.A. be taken away. Somehow the empty plastic picture frames on top of the Orocan drawers and the empty photo albums made her death even more real.

6.
Amah and my brother were watching WrestleMania when her leg went numb. Gua e sosi. Gua e sosi, she said, reaching out her hand to me as she was transferred to a gurney. My keys. My keys. Locking all the doors in the house was her night time routine. Without fail, she would put her keys on a plastic plate on top of the Orocan drawers before going to bed. And during the day, she would keep them in the front pocket of her duster, together with her handkerchief for her chronic sinusitis. She had left them on the plastic plate when she was rushed to the hospital that night. One week later, she was dead.

7.
Aren't all signs of death conjured up in hindsight when our mind tries so hard to connect the dots after a loved one's death? The signs, as people always say, are the unusual things the deceased do before they pass. Amah certainly gave out signs. She would never have stepped out of the house alone, much less gone for a walk. She would never have had her hair done by a different hairstylist, much less by a neighbor in the garage out in the open, where anyone could easily see her. She would never have watched a Bruce Lee movie on a computer, much less with earphones on because she was worried about her ears getting damaged. But all of this she did despite her fears.

8.
Wreaths and countless flowers from Amah's distant relatives filled the icy room. Amah used to tell me that friends would leave if you got no money to show for it or if you had nothing valuable to offer. Amah would always eat her bowl of congee with sweet potato alone for her 5 p.m. dinner.

On hot summer afternoons, she would douse her whole body with Green Cross alcohol and turn on the air conditioning. Every single day, she killed time playing solitaire with her dog-eared Bicycle playing cards made from cardboard. Before each game, she would pour Johnson's baby powder all over the cards, spread them across the bed, and slide them towards her in swift motions as she collected them in a deck. She would cut the deck in half and shuffle the cards repeatedly before laying them on the bed. This was her afternoon routine.

9.
Amah used to eat from a cereal bowl with yellow and blue squares arranged in grid-pattern composition around its shoulder. She only ate with a metal spoon, never with a fork or chopsticks. Before she got ready for dinner, she would change into her pajamas. She was wearing a white pair with dainty blue poppies days before she was rushed to the hospital. Mang tsap gua, I said to her out of spite when she invited me to have dinner with her. Ignore me. Don't bother me. Leave me alone. I was watching TV in the living room. She stood up, hitting the edge of the table with her body. And for the first time in her life, Amah, with all the nerves she could master that day, stormed out of the house and walked to my uncle's place four houses down the road, her metal spoon clinking against the cereal bowl as she left.

10.
If I had known then what I know now, I would have acted differently. They say that suffering in order to live to tell the story is costly. Amah, out of fear nurtured in war time, despised anything unfamiliar. How can you love and be with someone you can never understand? Her reluctance to try new things, her fear of going out of the house, her profound inability to assimilate to the local culture in Manila, and her annoyance at anything perceived as different seemed to mask this fear of the unknown. The way I acted, my dark skin, my broken Fukien, my taking after my father, my explosive laughter, my being maharot — or carefree — in my younger days shut me out into her unknown.

11.
Stress, the surgeon said when they asked him for the possible cause of the blood clot. My heart sank when I heard it. I couldn't help but think: Did

our argument cause her heart to pump more blood than usual, freeing the clot from somewhere deep in her system, like a rock dislodged from the earth by the sudden jolt of moving water? The chance that she would get well after the surgery was slim. It was still a chance nonetheless. After the surgery, which removed the blood clot, Saku and I stayed in the room with her. She was complaining about lower back pain. We thought they were bedsores, so I massaged her back with Johnson's baby powder. The doctor went inside the room, listened to her heart with a stethoscope, and left in haste.

12.
Amah was lying on a steel table in the hospital morgue. Her skin was still fair and she looked like she was sleeping. It must have been just a couple of hours. They said we needed to take out her dentures. My aunt couldn't, so I tried. I remember it vividly even now, more than a decade later. It shouldn't be a false memory, because I can remember the tightness of her dentures in her mouth as I tried to remove them. My brother and I were waiting outside in the hallway when Amah's heart suddenly gave out. But I remember it was an aorta that ruptured due to sudden blood flow that finally killed her. Did I massage her back too vigorously when I shouldn't have?

13.
The signs wouldn't have happened had we not fought. If she had not stormed out of the house, alone in her pajamas despite her fears, she wouldn't have invited me to take a stroll in the neighborhood. She wouldn't have asked for the neighbor's help to cut her hair. She wouldn't have said yes to me when I asked her to watch the Bruce Lee movie on the computer. And sometimes I can't help but think: If we hadn't fought, she wouldn't have died.

14.
It wasn't grief, Saku said when we talked about Amah's passing a decade later. He regretted the things he hadn't done and the things he hadn't done well enough. Saku gave me a piece of advice: Always be good to the people around you. Once they're gone, they'll never come back, no matter how many flowers you leave on their graves. The first time Amah suffered a stroke, my brother went sullen and quiet. The water motor broke down

and my brother had to fetch pails of water and climb up the stairs to water her plants on the balcony every single day, hoping that one day she would return and see her plants alive.

15.
For me, it was guilt. Amah used to grow aloe vera to keep her skin moisturized and her hair from falling out. She'd dab the aloe vera gel on her face, lips, and scalp every night. Days prior to her death, she asked me to transplant her young aloe vera plants to the yard, perhaps her way of trying to reach out to me. But I didn't. I had stopped spending time with her and, over time, I slowly forgot how to understand. Days after the burial, when everything had finally sunk in, I found myself bawling over her aloe vera plants as I carefully transplanted them in the yard.

16.
Inside the hospital, we basked in the artificial daytime from the bright lighting along the corridors, making time immeasurable. I fell into a kind of whirlpool of hoping and letting go. My guilt-ridden self made a bargain with God: If she came out alive, I would do everything to make her happy. My resentful self thought otherwise: But what if she woke up and told everyone that it's all my fault, like she always did whenever something terrible happened?

17.
Lola looks like she's sleeping, my 4-year-old cousin said when I lifted her up to see Amah's body inside the coffin. It was the first time I saw Amah with full makeup on. She was wearing a light beige blouse and skirt, which Tuaku, my first uncle, had bought her several years before. Lying there, she was smiling.

18.
There were only a few things that could make Amah feel at peace and happy: watching WrestleMania while eating boiled peanuts in bed, shopping for ballet flats, and folding and weaving paper animals. I would get excited whenever her light beige abanico fan frayed at the edges. That's when she would carefully undo the strips and fold them one on top of the other with her bony fingers until she turned them into a deer.

19.
Amah's passing is about losing the oldest member of the family, who possessed all the memories we could ever want to remember. It also meant losing our childhood home. Her last words before she died were never to go back to the old house. My brother and I didn't believe it — Amah loved that house. While she was still alive, she kept talking about going back and looking for her missing things. They sold the old house to a business owner, who turned it into a warehouse. On Google Maps, it looks abandoned and rundown. For us, her absence means one less person who can tell stories about our childhood.

20.
When I was young, on our way home from one of our road trips with Amah, I asked my cousin why the moon was following us. She said it's because it was big and far away. That time I couldn't grasp what she meant by that. Now that I'm older, I realize what it meant, especially for me. Amah's passing, no matter how distant it may seem, keeps creeping back to me: Golden pothos. Hibiscus. Aloe vera. Nescafé Classic. John Cena, The Rock, Warrior, and The Undertaker. Black cats with white bellies on the streets. Boiled peanuts. Dragonflies. Solitaire. Origami. The conch in my little cousin's bedroom. Woven paper deer.

21.
I don't have anything in my hands right now from Amah. What I do have is a woven deer made from strips of shredded manila folder. I taught myself how to make it from a Russian website. And strip by strip I wove them together as I tried to reconstruct Amah in my mind and what it meant to be someone who had always lived in the past. Letting go was non-negotiable in the art of losing someone.

22.
Dead people don't speak in dreams. I dreamt about Amah only once after her death. She was wearing her new yellow duster with tiny flowers she bought from Unimart-Greenhills Shopping Center. She was sleeping in her springy bed, her head resting on her arm, without a care in the world, as the sun flickered through the window, lighting up the whole room. Right then I knew we had finally found our peace.

The Overcoat
Leonid Newhouse

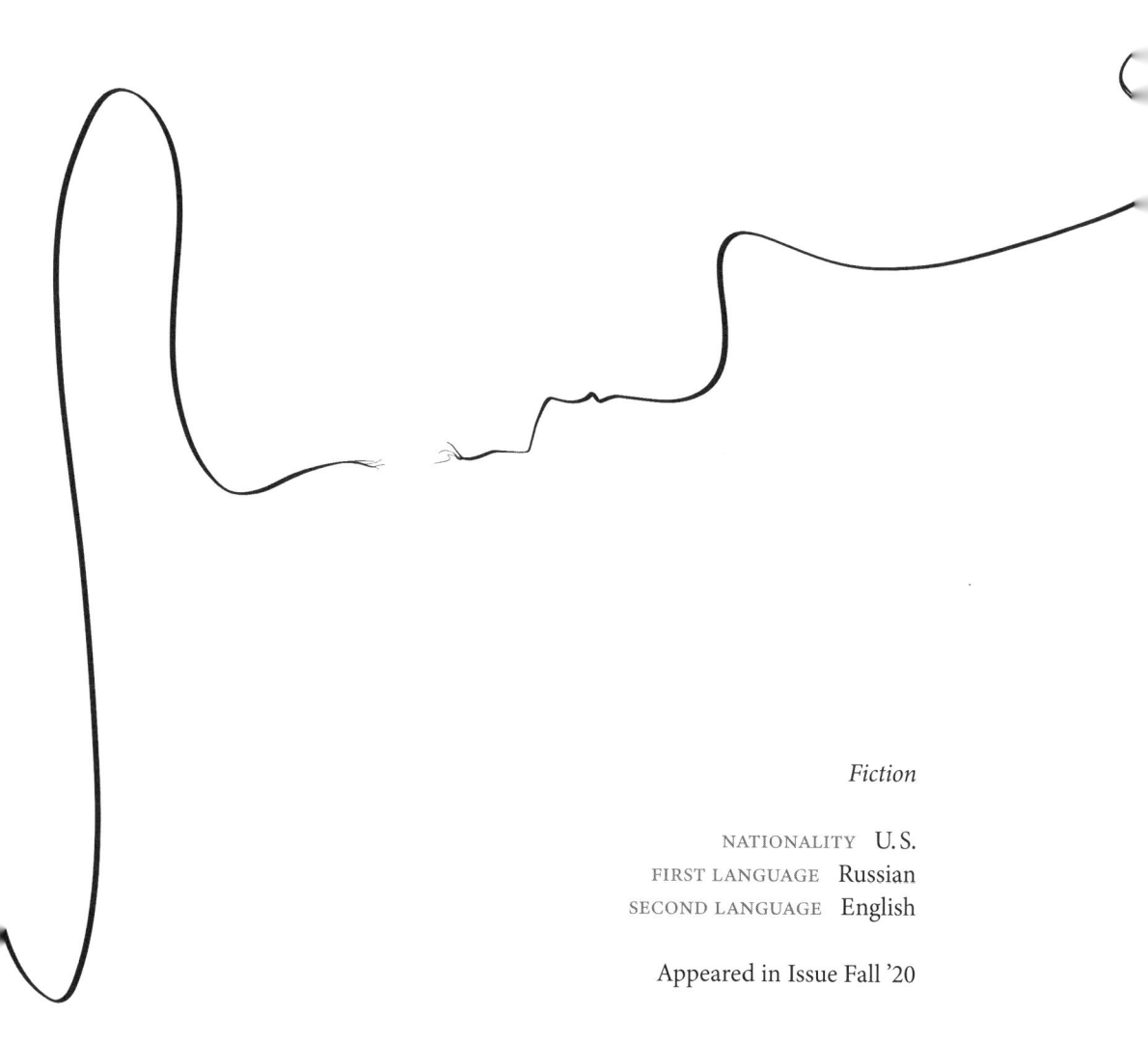

Fiction

NATIONALITY U.S.
FIRST LANGUAGE Russian
SECOND LANGUAGE English

Appeared in Issue Fall '20

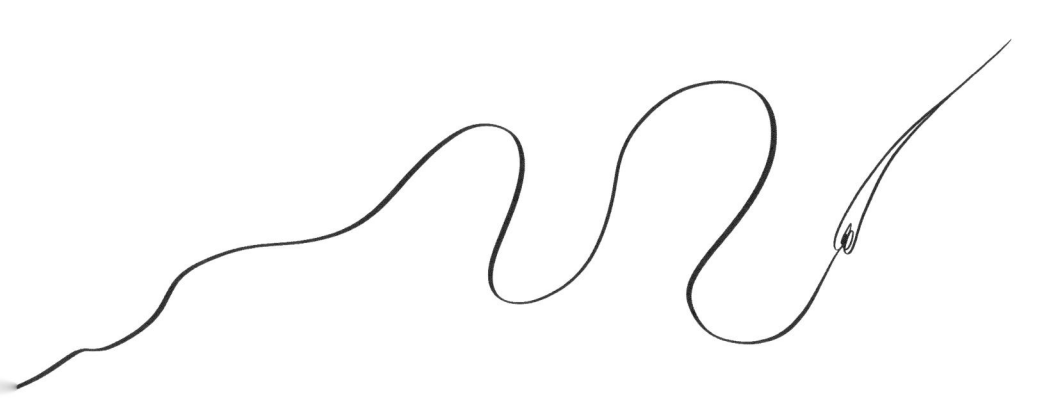

I stood by The Bronze Horseman and shivered. It was already April, but the frigid wind that blew in from the Neva went straight through me. Even Peter the Great, dressed as he was in his emperor's toga, looked chilled, his fingers of copper reaching stiffly toward the West.

Then I saw Yurek heading toward me across Decembrists' Square. Right away I noticed he was wearing a new coat. When he came closer, I saw what it was: a camel affair with lapels and sleeve flaps — the kind of coat an adult would wear. It made Yurek's slender, 14-year-old frame appear bigger and bulkier than usual. Even his normally pale face was a little flushed.

"Hey," I said. I wanted to tell him he was late but instead I only said, "Nice coat."

"Hey," he said, as if he didn't really care.

"Looks kind of fancy. Where's it made?"

"Poland."

Lucky bastard, I thought. Poland was almost Paris to us Soviets. My own coat, rough-hewn and threadbare, the color of the Leningrad sky in winter, was produced at a factory called "Bolshevichka." Naturally, I had already ripped off the tag with that shameful brand name, not that it made the coat look any better.

"Alright," I said, "let's get going."

"Let's — only I want to go up Nevsky."

For some time now, Yurek and I would get together after school and embark on a particular kind of expedition. We'd start by the horseman and trek along the Neva embankment, right by the Admiralty and the Hermitage Museum and the once-gorgeous palazzos, now state institutions with crumbling facades and bureaucratic titles etched on the tablets that hung by their entrances. We'd continue all the way to the Kirovskiy Bridge, then over to the opposite side of the river where the old battlecruiser Aurora and the bastions of the Peter and Paul fortress still grimly faced the Winter Palace — all the places we were most likely to bump into *zapadniki*, people from the West.

We were always on the lookout for Westerners. Our country was separated from the rest of the world by the mighty Iron Curtain, and visitors from the "other side" — in cold season, mostly Finns on coach tours — aroused in us no less curiosity than the first pale-faced arrivals must have among the natives of the New World. Everything about them was striking: their bright-colored outfits, the way they kept their heads up when they walked, like they weren't afraid of anything, even their chewing gum, that ultimate symbol of Western civilization that we craved. Each time we spotted one of their gleaming coaches, near some monument or museum, we would hide behind a granite column or a statue and wait for the mysterious representatives of the forbidden West to come out. I already knew some handy phrases, like "How do you do, sir!" and "Pleased to meet you!" I had learned in my English class that I was eager to use in "the real world." Yurek, who was bad with languages — the only thing he knew how to say was "*Purukummi yo*?" which meant "Got chewing gum?" in Finnish — appointed me to be our spokesman in any future head-to-head encounter with the aliens. But we could never find a way to get close enough to them without running the risk of being apprehended by the secret police — for the crime called "accosting foreigners" — so we usually admired them from afar.

"Why Nevsky?" I now asked Yurek. Nevsky Prospekt was Leningrad's main avenue. There were Westerners there too, of course, but there were also more police and more chances to get caught.

"I don't know," he shrugged. "It's kinda windy by the river, no?"

"But I thought your new coat was warm?"

"Not *that* warm."

"All right then," I conceded. "Nevsky it is."

We crossed over into Aleksandrovsky Gardens, its wooden benches vacant in anticipation of spring. The wind was blowing hard at our backs, pushing us forward, toward the Nevsky.

"How'd you come by the coat anyways?" I asked Yurek.

"Mom got it."

His mother, Aunt Ivanna, had stumbled upon the coat at the DLT department store. It was one of those rare occasions when a batch of imported coats suddenly arrived and a crowd of people elbowed and pushed their way to the counter. Luckily, Aunt Ivanna had in her pocket the child support money that Yurek's estranged father, Zorik, had sent her on the occasion of their son's 14th birthday.

"It's kinda big, your new coat, no?" I said.

"Not really." He straightened his back and spread out his shoulders. "It's supposed to be sort of loose anyway. That's how they wear them in the West."

He said it with so much authority I didn't dare to contradict him. Yurek was a couple years older, already in eighth grade, and I looked up to him, not least because I thought he was really lucky. He wasn't an only child like I was, but had a sister and a brother, with whom he lived in his mother's communal apartment on Pesochny Lane. The old bourgeois abode had winding, dimly lit hallways and old servants' quarters — a maid's room and a butler's pantry — adjacent to the kitchen. Yurek and his family occupied the former maid's room, an arrangement which, on account of its overcrowded condition, my mother used to call a "gypsy encampment," but whose rough conviviality I often envied. The communal pantry also had a nickname, *predbannik*, "the dressing room," given to it by Aunt Ivanna. She taught evening school, and Yurek and his siblings could do whatever they wanted all day after classes, which, to someone like me whose father was always on his case about homework, was the epitome of freedom. Late in the evening, the family would gather in *predbannik* to devour the sausage, cheese, and bread that Aunt Ivanna had picked up on the way from work — the fare that my mother dismissed as lowly "grub," but that I, with my mandatory warm supper, secretly craved.

Then there was Yurek's pale complexion. He wasn't swarthy like me, but had straw-colored hair with a golden sheen and big blue eyes of a good-natured rascal that he inherited from his father, Zorik. And even though he also had Zorik's aquiline nose that would ultimately earn him, among friends, the nickname Pelican, no one ever called him *zhid* at the pioneer camps where we summered. Yurek's "Aryan" looks, together with his Polish surname, Chernyavsky, fooled the young anti-Semites with red bandannas around their necks into believing that he was a fellow Slav.

And now he had this sporty new coat.

As usual, Nevsky was full of commotion. Throngs of passersby in drab attire moved past shop windows with displays of domestic things that no one wanted. Yurek's coat stood out in the crowd, and I noticed girls give him quick, stealthy once-overs. I realized that Yurek must have picked Nevsky on purpose. Everybody who wore imported stuff would take it to Nevsky sooner or later.

But there were no Westerners in sight. We had already passed by all the likely landmarks — the House of Books, the Kazansky Cathedral, the Anichkov Palace — and still not a single shiny coach!

"Where the hell did they all go?" I heard Yurek mutter.

"To the Hermitage, I bet," I said, "or else, to the Fortress." I now felt mad that we had taken the Nevsky route, instead of our usual one along the river, where we never failed to see at least a few foreign buses. *Just because he wanted to show off that stupid coat of his!*

We were now at Vosstaniya Square mall with its metro station in the shape of a rotunda with columns, a crowd of gypsies, winos, and idlers milling around. Stone markers linked with heavy cast-iron chains separated the mall from the rest of the square. This was where the "fashionable" part of Nevsky ended and the seedier one began. Behind the markers, across Ligovsky Prospekt loomed the facade of the Oktyabrskaya Hotel, where my mother worked as concierge of the fourth floor. In the warmer months the sidewalk before the hotel was crowded and there were many buses and cars parked in front of it, but now it was all but empty.

We were about to call it a day and split, when a big, red-and-blue coach pulled up in front of the Oktyabrskaya. "See that?" said Yurek.

"Yeah!"

"Let's go and check it out." And he started in the direction of the hotel.

"Wait," I said. "Wait."

"What?"

"Why don't we watch them from around here? We could hide behind one of these columns."

"No, I want to get close. Maybe we could get some gum."

"But..." No one was supposed to loiter in front of hotels like Oktyabrskaya where foreigners stayed. The only time I went near the hotel was when I visited my mother. I would go in through the back entrance, where the guard knew me. My mother had told me that the hotel had a special office called *piket*, staffed with KGB men, *piketchiki*, whose job was to detain anyone they suspected of accosting foreigners. "What if we get caught?"

"We'll just walk past the coach. We could be living around the corner from the hotel. We have the right to walk home, no?"

His argument satisfied me. I followed him as he made his way through the crowd. Some Romany women tried to grab our hands and tell us our fortunes but we brushed them aside. We stepped over the cast-iron chain and crossed Ligovsky Prospekt. The facade of the Oktyabrskaya rose before us like a castle. We began to walk alongside the hotel toward the red-and-blue coach.

It was a double-decker with a windshield that extended almost all the way down to the bumper, which made it look like a spaceship. Its diesel engine idled expectantly and a greyhound raced along its sleek flank. The sign above the windshield read: *Turku–Helsinki–Leningrad*. The uniformed driver slumped back in his captain's seat, a pair of gold-rimmed sunglasses on his nose, his jaws masticating. I smiled at him, but he screwed his nose and looked away.

Yurek and I circled the coach as if it were a monument; we admired its massive wheels, its tinted windows, and the three-point silver star on its radiator. Mercedes-Benz! That they employed the most prestigious automotive marque in the world as a means of public transportation was most awesome. Nobody in the Soviet Union, with the exception of the General Secretary Brezhnev, rode in a Mercedes. Even the fumes the coach emitted seemed to have a sweet, aromatic smell, which I inhaled with pleasure.

"Bet they'll be coming out any minute," said Yurek.

"Who?" I said, momentarily dizzy from the fumes.

"The Finns, who else."

I looked toward the front entrance of the hotel. A burly doorman stood behind the glass front door, his hands behind his back, yawning. The pale sun was already setting behind the new Concert Hall to the west, and the puddles on the sidewalk had a black film of ice. This was the last place on earth I'd want to be caught accosting foreigners, I thought. Then the sun hit the glass door, and I could no longer see the doorman.

I tugged at the flap of Yurek's sleeve. "We better go," I said. "There's that doorman over there."

Yurek pushed my hand away. He examined the flap and smoothed it over with his hand. "You chickening out?" he said.

"Me? No!"

"Here they come!"

Yurek raised the collar of his coat; he now looked like an overblown spy, lacking only sunglasses. We quickly positioned ourselves near the door of the coach. "Don't forget," he said, "you have to say something first."

"I will," I promised, so nervous I felt I could throw up. Or was it the fumes?

But the Finns were already filing past us, tall and lanky, looking as exotic as well-dressed giraffes. The scent of their deodorized bodies and peppermint-flavored breaths made me delirious. All the English phrases I knew became jumbled in my head.

"Come on," Yurek poked me with his elbow, "say *something*!"

"OK, OK." I spotted a middle-aged man who smiled at me. "How d-do you do, sir!" I stuttered.

The man parted his hands and shook his head, as if to say, "I have nothing."

"Damn," Yurek cursed, shifting from one foot to the other. "He didn't get what you said."

"Why don't you talk to them yourself then?"

There were only a few Finns left in the line. One of them was a tall blond woman in furs. Yurek stepped toward her. "*Purukummi yo*?" he mumbled.

The woman stopped and patted him on the head, then quickly pressed something into his hand.

In a moment all the Finns had boarded the coach, which gave a blast of black smoke and took off. When the diesel cloud had settled, Yurek opened his hand. A thick package of Wrigley's Citron rested gloriously upon his palm. *Lemon flavor!* The bright-yellow nugget gleamed as if made of pure gold. Lucky bastard, I thought again.

"Gotcha," a hoarse voice growled over our heads. It was the doorman. He had sneaked up on us, and now we were caught red-handed. He grabbed Yurek by the shoulders and lifted him up like a puppy. "I'll teach you how to pester foreigners, punk!" And he began to drag Yurek toward the front entrance.

Yurek struggled frantically to extricate himself from the doorman's grip. His feet skipped against the ground, like those of a cartoon character, and his arms thrashed the air.

"Let go of me, uncle!" he pleaded. "Let go!"

"Not for anything!" And the doorman yanked hard at Yurek's arm.

There was a crackling sound, and as Yurek broke free, I saw something dangle in the doorman's paw like a dead rat.

We ran, followed by the doorman's loud curses.

Behind the Concert Hall we dove into a doorway. The dim stairway reeked of cats and stale borscht. We ran up a few flights of stairs and stopped at a landing with a cracked, dirty window, breathing hard. Yurek held his left shoulder as if nursing a wound.

"My sleeve," he moaned. "It's gone!"

He looked so pale one would have thought he had lost his whole arm.

"The doorman must have got it," I said.

"That motherfucker."

Yurek took off his coat and held it up against the light from the window, turning it this way and that and shaking his head. He was wearing two layers of sweaters underneath. His mother must have got the coat a size or two larger, figuring it would last him longer that way. Yurek, who was tall for his age but very thin, had had to put on those sweaters as padding for the extra room in the chest and shoulders. That's what had given him that bulky, puffed-up look.

"I wonder what he did with the sleeve," he said at length.

"Probably gave it to the *piket*, as evidence or something."

"Damn!"

There was silence. Yurek looked so crestfallen I thought he might start to cry any moment. But then he swallowed hard and said, "I got to get it back."

"Really? Like how?"

"I don't know. I'll go back to the hotel, whatever."

"What, are you crazy?"

He looked at me strangely and repeated, "I'll go back and get it."

"But you'll end up in the *piket*!" I objected. "They'll notify our parents. My father might beat me up." My father hadn't beaten me since I was in first grade, but, given the gravity of the offense, he might pull out his old army belt and give me a thrashing.

"And my mother," said Yurek, "will *kill* me if I come home without the sleeve." He told me how his mother had waved a rolling pin at his older brother, Sasha, when Sasha had swapped his leather shoes for a pair of Chinese-made sneakers. "And now she'll be really mad, 'cause my father won't be giving her any money again for a long time."

I had no idea that Aunt Ivanna ever hit her sons. I knew that when she came home at night with a bad headache, they would scatter around the apartment and not come out until she had taken her aspirin. Still Yurek was her favorite and I still remembered the times when she would sit him on her lap and pat him on the head and call him *kotik*, her little kitten, and Yurek would purr happily. I now had second thoughts about Yurek's good luck.

We sat down on the well-worn steps. It was getting dark.

"Think your mother could get it back for me?" Yurek said.

"Well…" I knew that my mother often felt bad for the Chernyavsky kids, because of the circumstances they lived in, and because their father had left them. Naturally, she wouldn't want Yurek to get in trouble. But I didn't necessarily want to tell my mother about our mischief. I knew she wouldn't take kindly to it.

"I mean, she must know all those *piketchiki*, right?"

"Yes, but…"

"Look," he said, "she'll find out anyway. When I come home and tell my mom how I lost that sleeve, the first thing she'll do is call your mother."

That was true; our mothers spoke on the phone every day. They had no secrets from each other.

"I'll tell you what," he continued. "Why don't you talk to your mom? Maybe she could get it settled and sew the sleeve on, and then my mother won't even know."

He was right. It was better that I tell my mother myself than have Aunt Ivanna call her. "OK," I said. "I'll go talk to her. Wait for me inside the metro station."

Yurek nodded meekly and handed me his coat. Without it he looked smaller and less self-assured, his two layers of sweaters notwithstanding.

"Just make sure to ask her not to tell my mom," he said.

"Don't worry." I rolled the coat up. I had to hold it with both my arms, like a baby. "It's pretty bulky, your coat," I said, and headed back to the hotel.

My mother sat behind her desk at the end of a long corridor. Hers was a strange job. Officially, she gave out keys and managed room attendants, but she was also supposed to be a snoop, reporting to *piketchiki* on anyone who loitered around or visited foreigners in their rooms. Her desk's strategic position at the end of the corridor allowed her to see straight down the whole length of the floor. Because of that she knew all the *piketchiki* — just as Yurek had suggested. She was sitting alone behind the desk, her silvery chignon gleaming in the light of the desk lamp. My mother's hair had begun to turn gray when she was still in her twenties.

"Pretty business you got yourselves into," she said when I finished my story. "You both have grown big but you don't have any brains in your heads."

I listened patiently, knowing from experience that the best thing to do was to say nothing and look guilty, so I pursed my lips and stared at the tips of my shoes.

"So what do you expect me to do now?" she asked.

"Maybe you could get Yurek's sleeve from the *piket*?" I said. I also wanted to ask her if she would sew the sleeve back onto Yurek's coat, but decided to wait until later.

My mother shook her head incredulously. "Where do you think that would leave *me*?"

I kept staring at my shoes. I knew my mother could get anything if she really wanted it. She was on familiar terms with a lot of people, including the director of the hotel himself. She always arranged rooms and airline tickets and other favors for friends and acquaintances. My mother had the right way with people in power.

"I'll tell you what," she said. "You both deserve a good thrashing, that's for sure." Then she reached for the phone.

"Ivan Borisych, dear," she said, smiling at the invisible head of the *piket*. My mother never talked so sweetly with me or with my father, only with other people, especially those from whom she wanted something. When she talked like that with other men, I sometimes felt bad for my father, for both of us. But now I didn't mind. "May I stop in?"

She put the phone down, and the smile left her face. "Wait for me here," she ordered, and headed toward the elevator.

I sat and waited for her, gazing down the endless corridor with identical doors on both sides. I thought about my father coming home from work and eating his supper alone. I knew he would worry about me and all the homework that remained undone. And he'd probably worry about my mother, too. He hated her working night shifts and not being around at suppertime.

I'd tell my father everything, I decided — but not about how my mother talked with Ivan Borisych.

When my mother returned from the *piket* with the severed sleeve in her hand, her face seemed impenetrable. She sewed the sleeve back on with quick, practiced strokes, like a surgeon. Later she wrapped the mended coat in some old newspapers and ushered me out through the back door. "Don't get yourself into any more trouble now," she admonished.

It was already nighttime. In the cold glare of the streetlights Vosstaniya Square looked semi-deserted. All the fortune tellers and winos were gone.

I crossed over Ligovka back toward the metro station, the ice on the puddles crunching under my shoes. Then I stepped over the chain barrier and went into the station.

Yurek was standing in the corner of the vestibule. In his two layers of sweaters he looked like a homeless boy. I handed him the package with his coat, and he unwrapped it and examined it carefully. My mother had done a fine job; you couldn't even tell the coat had been repaired. It looked like new again.

"Did you ask her not to tell my mom?" Yurek said.

"Yeah."

"Good." He put on the coat and raised the collar. He looked perfectly cocky again.

"I better get going," he said. "See you tomorrow."

"See you."

I watched him walk home, across the empty mall, to his dinner of sausage, cheese, and bread.

The Brother Moves On
Sihle Ntuli

Poetry

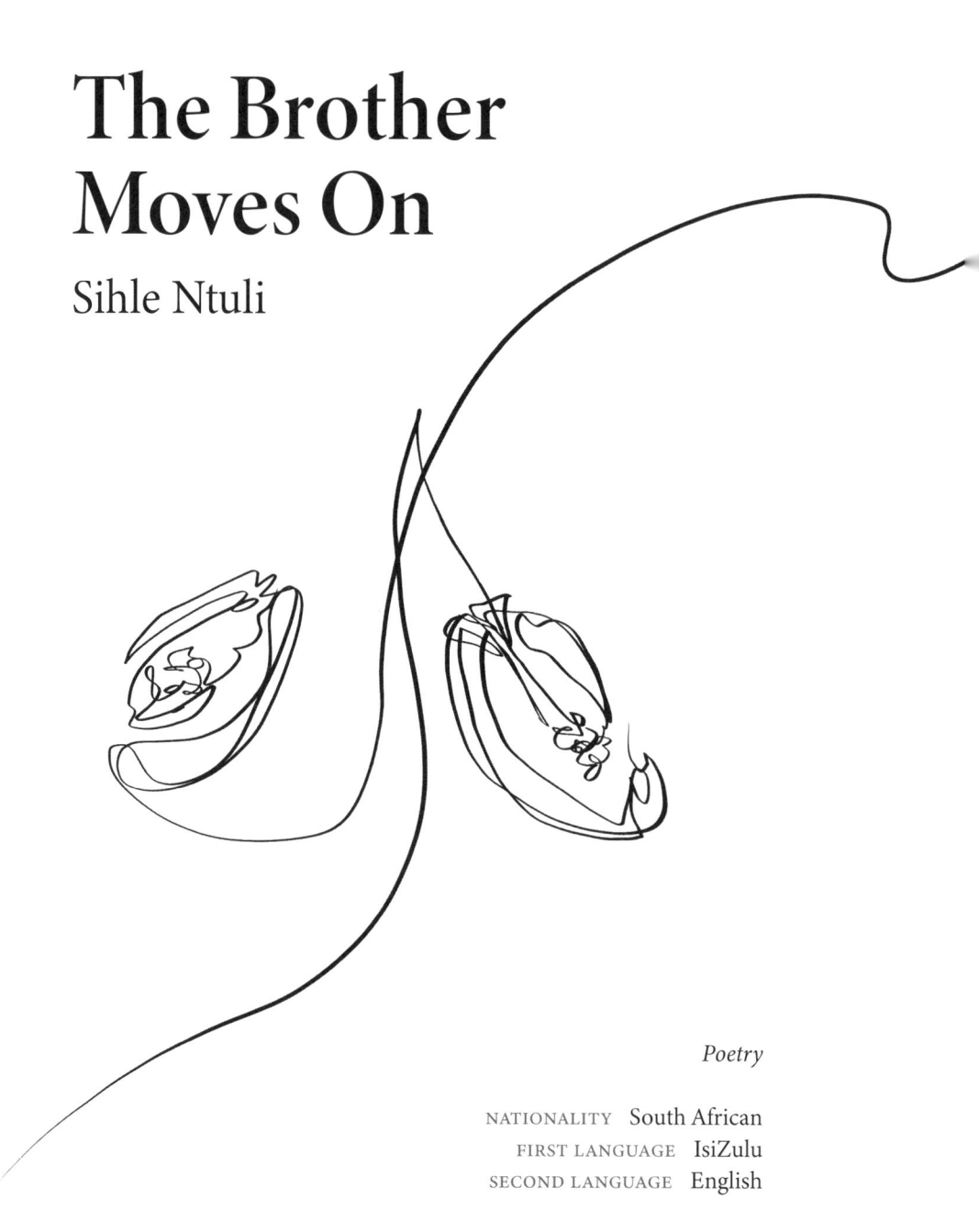

NATIONALITY South African
FIRST LANGUAGE IsiZulu
SECOND LANGUAGE English

Appeared in Issue Fall '20

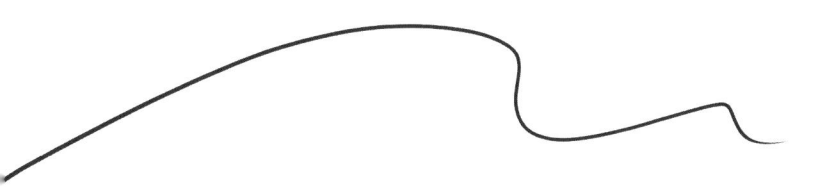

Do you remember
    when we were younger,
   ugogo gathering pawpaw from her garden,
   sitting patiently waiting
   for us to finish indulging in the fruit,
   knowing full well
     that her grandsons
   would only want more,
   and with the very last one,
    she plunged the knife deep inside
    in two,
The way she sat close by
    and watched us
     tasting rich textures
    of a tropical delicacy,
   and once we had our fill she imparted wisdom
     on the necessity to share
   with one another,
Reminding us,
   that when we entered this world
    we entered it together as twins
   amawele
     and that twins
    was how God had intended it to be
   that you and I were born this way for a reason.

Lest we forget
      her lesson in the garden
      much later in life,   I would learn
      that our late grandmother   decided on our names
      in much the same way,
      after   you entered   this world   first
      it was ugogo   who decided,
      that my name
            would be on the end of yours
As a reminder,
      that even when we separate
            we will remain together always.
    brother,
      I know
      how life
      can often
      feel like
      years
      of accumulating
          soil
      burying us alive,
and on that day in the garden
I felt   the words
of our grandmother,
          as her bare hands
          in brown soil
          delicately
          placed a seed
          deep
              within us,
          in a place
          where hope can live
her hope
      that someday
      a soaring tree   with leaves   protruding
      from tender parts
      of the chest,

        a bond   as strong
        as the oak tree
              that towers over
              providing shade
              from a harsh sun,
        and so, brother
                    with this in mind
        I must ask you   once more,
Do you remember?

Cuminte
Adriana Onița

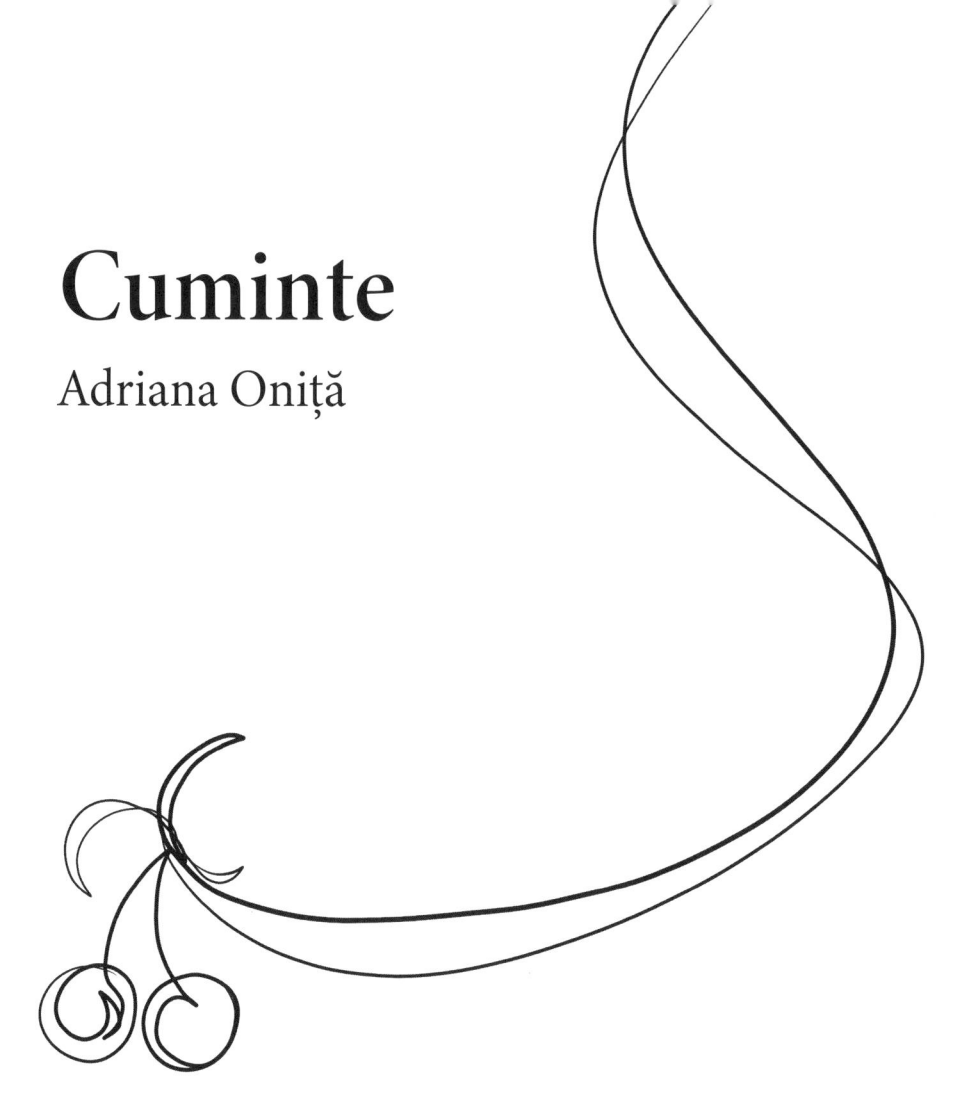

Poetry

NATIONALITY Romanian & Canadian
FIRST LANGUAGE Romanian
SECOND LANGUAGES English, Spanish, French & Italian

Appeared in Issue Spring '23

I carry you, Rafael, like I carry drafts
of poezii in română și spaniolă,
like I carry grief, dor, rugăciuni.

You've carried me across
livezi de vișini, lilac groves, grotte,
fields of *eu* to become *noi*.

For you, *I* doesn't exist.
Noi suntem *noi*, we are new
to this surrender. We enter
the ravine alone, împreună.
We gather bouquets of creeping bellflower,
yellow toadflax, tufted vetch.

Even when I thought I was *I*,
ai fost cu mine. Ai fost cuminte.
Cu minte, with my mind, like when
we painted those crooked trees, and
sang while biking to Torre Sibiliana.
You were a pomegranate seed.

Să fii cuminte. First time you go
into a ravine alone, don't even
tell me. Trust our hemispheres—
the way out of the lilac grove
is through livada de vișini.

When Romanian parents urge their kids to be "cuminte," this can mean: be good, be quiet, be kind, be careful, be polite, be smart, or be obedient. I wrote this poem for my newborn son, Rafael Mihai, returning to the original root of the word (cu + minte) to remind him of how we will always be connected with our minds.

Dogs
Giada Pesce

Winner of the Readers' Choice Award

Poetry

NATIONALITY Italian
FIRST LANGUAGE Italian
SECOND LANGUAGE English

Appeared in Issue Fall '22

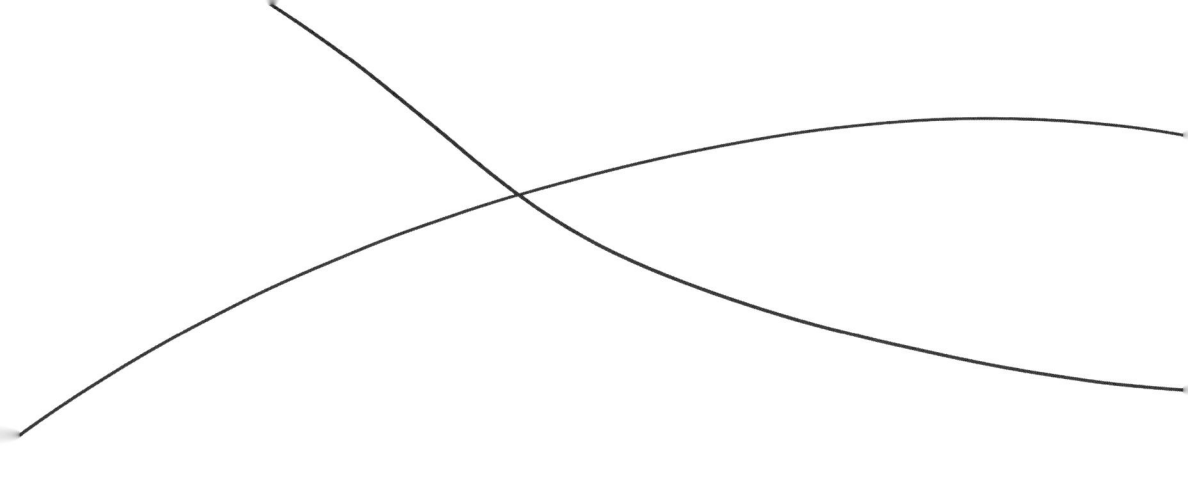

Is it that dream you sell?
Of that day when I was eight
and I was running with the dogs?

Down those stairs the steps so wide
my soles slapped the pavement

crushing that lizard away
from its wiggling tail,
blood drops drawn around the frenzy of its dance.

A summer echo around the smell of warm silence
while the sun pounded with sweat in my ears,

ponytail swaying side to side,
dog nails screeching,
and the screaming concrete.

Is it this dream you sell?
Is it that smell of home,
the water running brown with soap,
talcum powder on my back?

Running from boys that night,
the steps still so wide.

When he spat in my hair
there were no dogs in sight.

It's Like a Curry Sandwich

Skanda Prasad

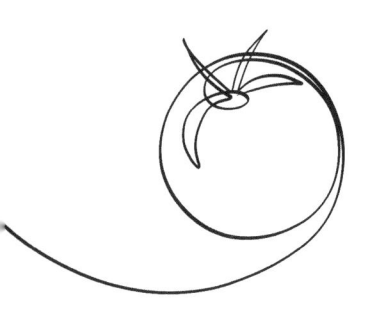

Poetry

NATIONALITY Indian
FIRST LANGUAGE Kannada
SECOND LANGUAGES English & Hindi

Appeared in Issue Fall '20

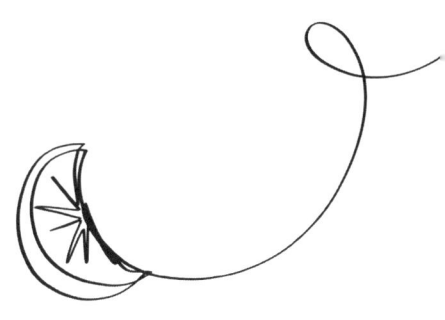

I
Bengaluru, 1994

Amma never made this at home,
and Grandma — bless her heart —
would've fainted at the touch
of the proscribed onions,
but ever so rarely we'd traipse
to the *chaat* shop,

uncurl our fists from gnarled fingers,
point a chopstick digit, toothpick-length,
at the chalkboard menu and ask
for pubbuhjee. *Appa*'s moustache
always smiled

before his lips did,
translated child-talk
to the cashier I mistook
for a rapper when he screamed
over the kitchen clangs

One masala dosa one idli two coffee two badam milk one upma
and two paav bhaaji, forty-six rupees please.

II
Paav Bhaji
Bread and cooked veggies.

First, the boiling: Potatoes,
conquistador trophies from Peru,
rotund constancies, first fit
only for cattle,
                then, the poor;

peas, cauliflower, and carrots,
bouquets from the Fertile Crescent —
Middle East, Cyprus, Persia.

Then, the sautéing. Baptise in angry oil
cumin from the Levant, onions, garlic,
ginger from Nusantara; chillies and
capsicum, fiery shells of the Columbian
Exchange, and tomatoes
red like Aztec blood; hissing
aroma assailing the house, settling
on next month's clothes.

Step three. The bubbling of the stew:
Vegetables — julienned, smashed, diced,
boiled, quartered, regressed to inchoateness,
New World and Old coalesced in roils
of butter; unblanded by salt and spices:
cinnamon, turmeric, cardamom, and black
pepper — the Indian heart of the dish —
Moluccan cloves, Iraqi fenugreek,
and dried chillies, suffusing
into each other
like a murmuration of starlings

and crowned with a grove of cilantro,
lime, and tearfully shredded onions
atop *ghee*-toasted rolls of well-risen bread.

III
'Pav Bhaji'
Paõ: Bread — from the Portuguese patois

of Vasco da Gama, First Count
of Vidigueira, Second Viceroy of India,
Admiral of the Seas of Arabia, Persia,
India and *all* the Orient, discoverer
of routes known to Arabs, Indians,
and Chinese
           only for millennia;

who, in search of *'Christians
and spices'*, misheard *Krishna* as Christ,
thought temples were bastard churches,
and the natives, lost Catholics;

who, when laughed out of court for his gifts
to the *Samoothiri* of Malabar — sugar, oil,
honey, six hats, and four scarlet cloaks —
decided to help himself
to sixteen fishermen — savages,
bravely seized — as he decamped
from God's own country.

He must've liked the taste enough
for a bigger helping on the second sojourn:
Arab trade ships, fishing villages, factories,
lips and ears of a Hindu priest — the same one
who'd introduced him to the Malabar King —
helpfully replaced with the ears of a dog,

and four-hundred pilgrims,
Mecca-bound, looted, beaten,
locked in their ship, and burnt to a crisp:

fish folk, coolies, mothers squeezing their babies
through red-hot portholes, merchants, cooks

stewing vegetables — *Bhaji* — for dinner
after the evening prayers, genuflections
towards a land they'd never see.

IV
Atlanta, 2017

'Paav Bhaajee'

Ordered one, this time with clear vowels,
clenched jaw, and the extra sprinkle
of *Americanese*, so I'd be understood
when asking for cheese on top

No rap waiter this time, just a kid,
Aum tattoo and coifed moustache,
greeting us with *namaste y'all*, mangling
the names — I made him repeat
Sev Bataataa Dahi Puri five times
for a laugh, stretched out

till the check arrived
with my chai *latte*.

I taught myself to cook
Paav Bhaji the next day.

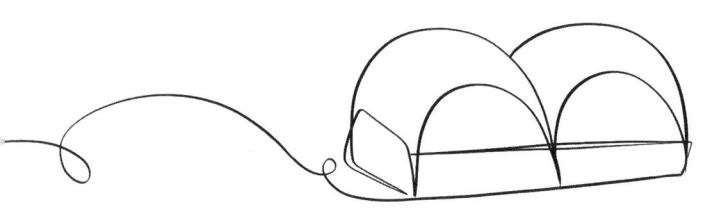

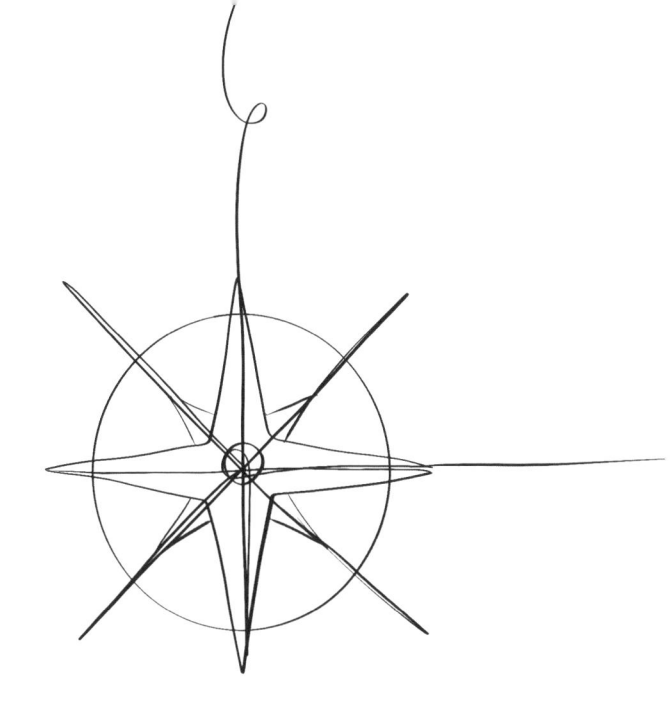

Sito

Laura Theis

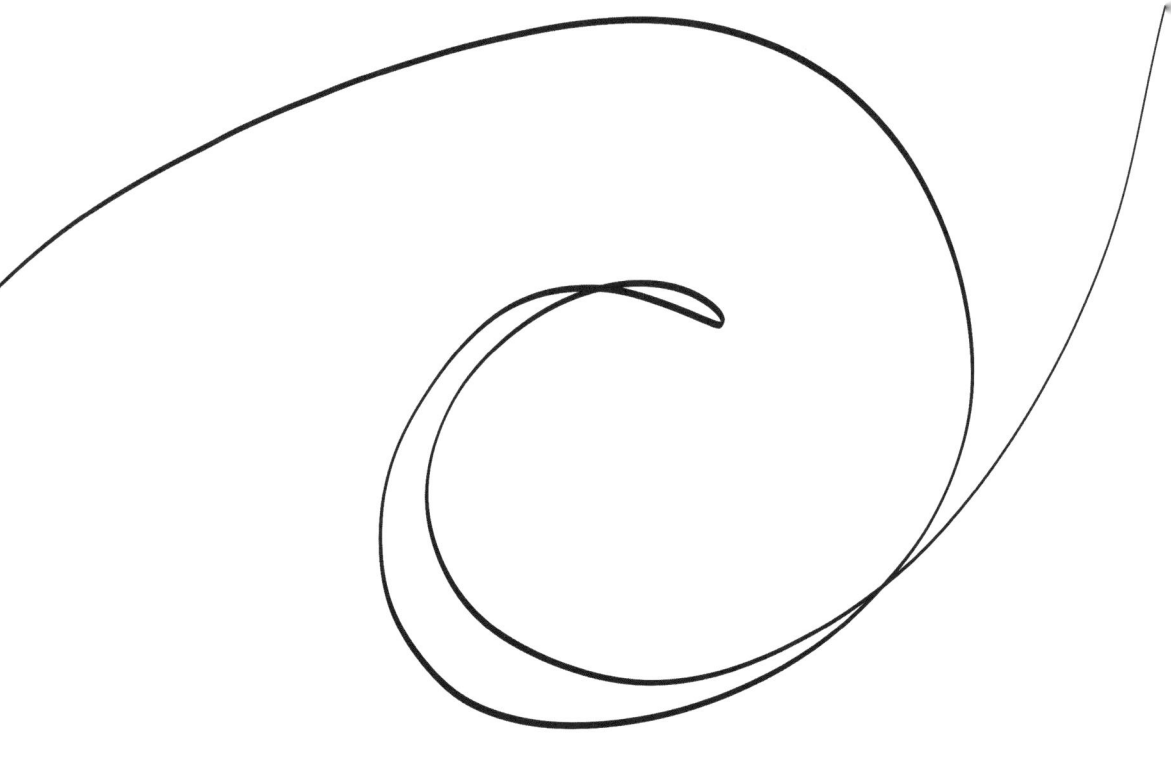

Poetry

NATIONALITY German
FIRST LANGUAGE German
SECOND LANGUAGE English

Previously unpublished

how could I ever bring myself to say
that it may never happen

how could I tell you about bread and fear,
a feast of solitude

how could I ever prepare you to tell
the women from the pain

when you ask me what weighs heavier
the feather or the fog

when you ask to sing of what spring might be
the dream of the flower loaf

forgive me not only for the silence but also
for what this silence suggests

the distance is an audible frost
one note held which once lost

turns to silver
I promise

I cannot teach you more than this winter desert
the cold sands hold the same knowledge with more eloquence

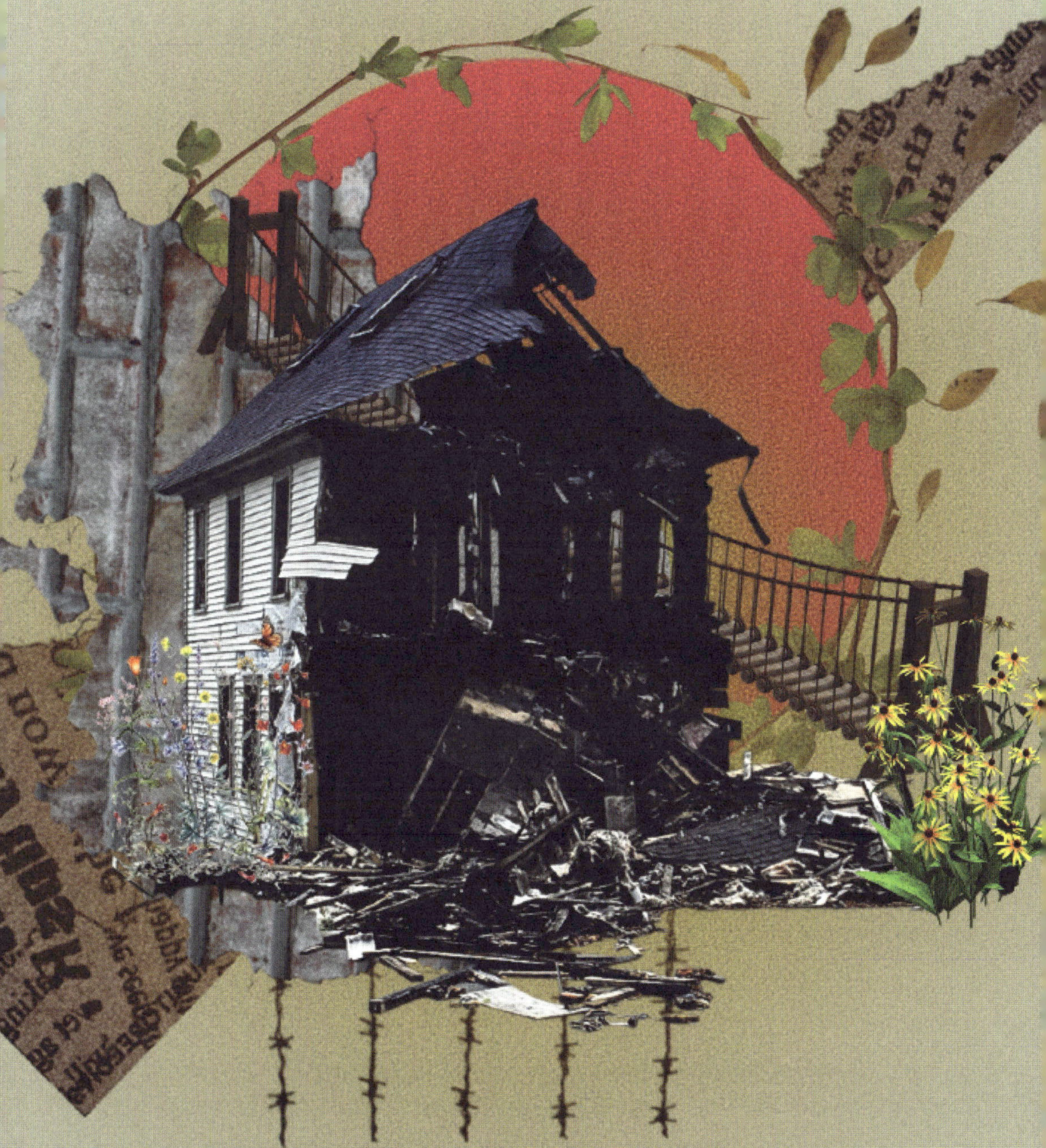

(IM)MIGRATION

Migrating is a painful experience. There can be no painless leaving of one's home and homeland. Some people are driven out of their country by force. Some leave out of frustration or necessity. Some simply to change up their lives, to breathe in fresh air after years of inhaling miasmic vapors. Yet, the pain is there. There can be no painless leaving of one's home and homeland. The rip into one's existence that migrating and immigrating produce can never heal. This is part of the story told in the works collected here: the bitter sarcasm of "Immigrant Sitcom"; the bleak disillusionment of "When We First Arrived, 1983"; the "familiar ache" of a forever foreign world as described in "Otherland."

These texts contain much more than pain though. They contain the whole impressive arc of lifetimes that have seen and known and dealt with a lot more than they ever bargained for. The simple truth of thinking and saying, "I am an immigrant," this blinding, sudden realization constitutes a point of no return. The following stories deal with new possibilities, discovered identities, and the dream of financial stability. After all, the primary motive behind immigrating is to improve one's life. It leads one to become part of an "imagined [...] community" — to use Benedict Anderson's famous definition — one that becomes the teeming environment of a life that needs to be rebuilt from the ground up.[8]

Migrating is the ultimate journey. The pieces collected in this anthology show the reader sharp sketches from personal odysseys. To quote the late poet Charles Simic from the foreword to another anthology of translingual writing, "If you wish to have an interesting life, become an immigrant or a refugee."[9] The self-assurance of such a statement might seem overreaching, but — as Simic knew, as I know, and as the writers collected here know — both the clear and subterranean implications of such a move are hard to overstate and even harder to avoid. Immigrating becomes, without exception, the single most consequential fact of a life. It brings with it the awareness of one's worth and dignity, even in the face of fear and alienation, of crushing loneliness and racist discrimination.

This might even be truer for writers who immigrated, their artistic selves split into a plurality. As immigrant writer Edvige Danticat puts it, "the language you were born speaking and the one you will probably die speaking *have no choice* but to find a common place in your brain and regularly merge there."[10] This forced merging of languages, cultures, and identities produces unique works. Writers, artists, and poets, with their heightened sensitivities and sense of self, see their craft seismically changed by the move. Others find the first bud of their art pushing out of the soil left in its wake. The texts presented here help give their readers a deeper understanding of (im)migration, opening their minds to one of the most obvious and mysterious circumstances of an increasingly large number of lives.

by Filippo Bagnasco

No Place Called Home

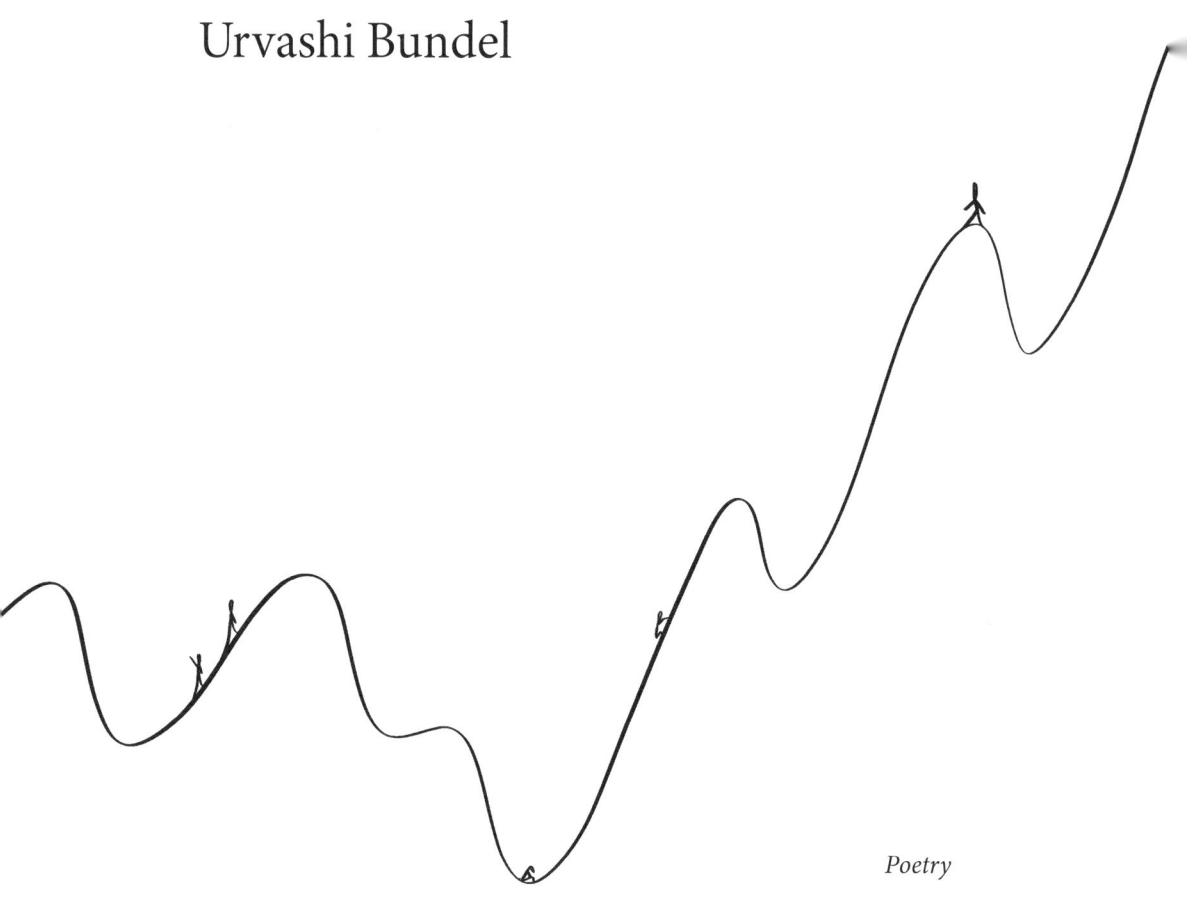

Urvashi Bundel

Poetry

NATIONALITY   Indian
FIRST LANGUAGE   Hindi
SECOND LANGUAGES   English, Urdu & Japanese

Previously unpublished

Written in honor of the stateless people from the Rakhine state in Myanmar, fleeing Myanmar in search for a better identity. The prose is based on real-life conversations with the Rohingyas.

We left rejected from their homelands,
Became homeless.
We left dejected from their homelands,
Became spiritless.
Alienated, we stood in the marshy wastelands of Cox's Bazar,
Deprived, we sat in dilapidated corners of the Rakhine,
Of Tang Ma Road, where we carried heavy boulders on our shoulders,
Heavy with hatred and demented in faith,
We carried on dismissed ancestral chains,
Heavy with crimson-colored soil from our backyards,
We stood for a family photograph, each year —
Our siblings' names get crisscrossed in haste and anger,
By the tyrannical army, with pens, soaked in brother's blood,
Dejected, stand silent in the smoky valleys of Maungdaw,
Of Kaung Daung, where sugar plantations bore no sugar in our life,
We toiled under the barbed wires and scorching heat,
Burned while crossing borders,
Our sisters hid in brutally raped dungeons,
Burned, we ran toward unchartered shores of Australia,
Singing the folklores that our mothers sang to us,
We swim with courage, but no identity,
Toward wandering alleys of New Zealand,
And makeshift domiciles of Kutupalong.
We fled from no human saving our rights,
We fled without protection, humanness, or knight,
We fled from nightmares that came to life, each morning,
We fled from the cannibalism that played at our doorsteps, each night,
Shunned, we lament for a place called, home.
So we swim with courage, but no identity.

Otherland
Edvige Giunta

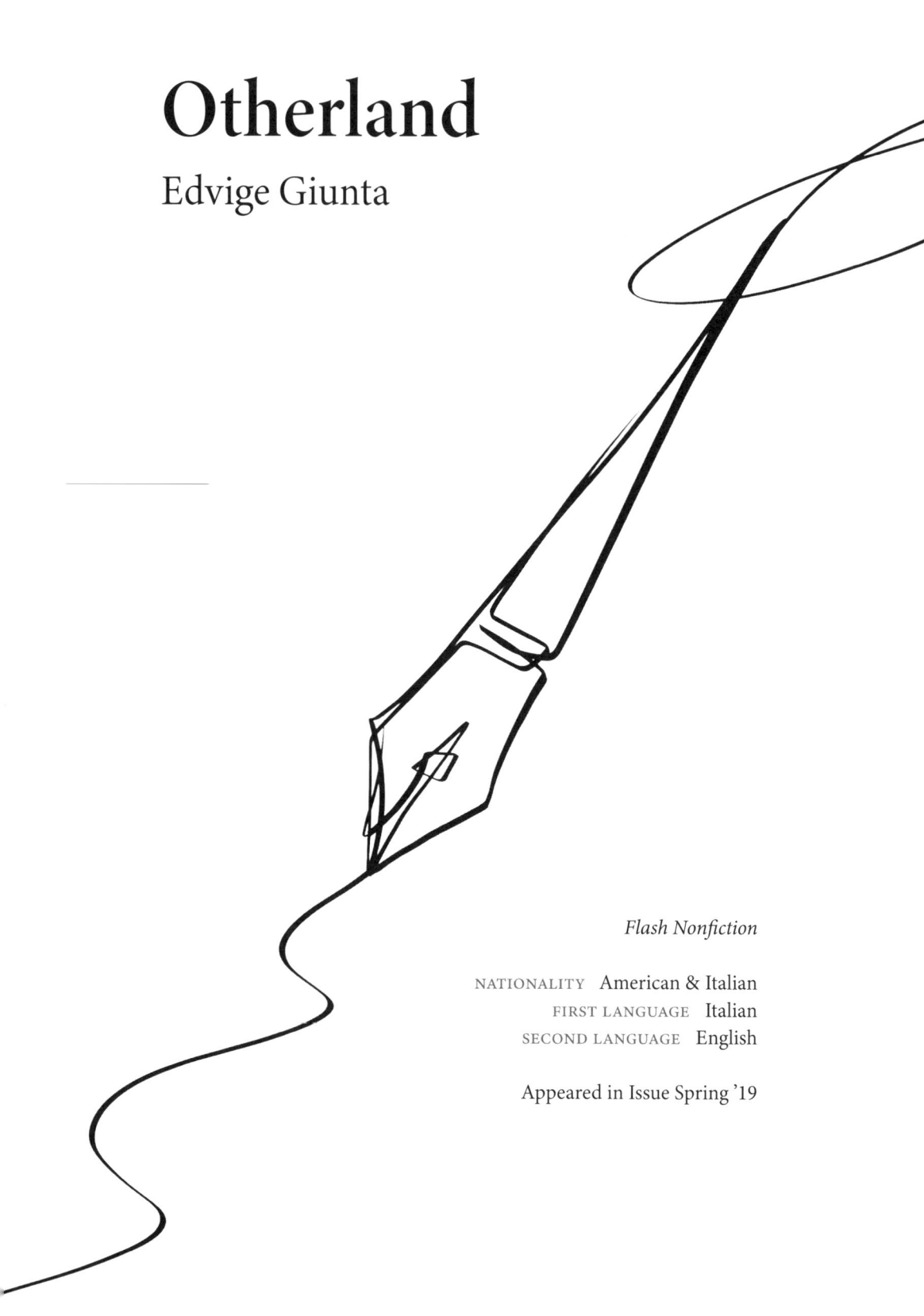

Flash Nonfiction

NATIONALITY American & Italian
FIRST LANGUAGE Italian
SECOND LANGUAGE English

Appeared in Issue Spring '19

Homesickness grows like a weed. I consider Spain a suitable candidate for my next home. I fantasize about living in a small house overlooking the Mediterranean, where I will write, the humming of waves in my ears.

At night I will watch planets and stars, clear in the undisturbed sky. On the plane of reluctant returns, the chatter of the Sicilian girlfriend of my adolescence stays in my head. Images of falling asleep with my mother, of wandering through the streets of old Catania, of stopping to buy freshly picked figs and berries from a crate sitting on a rickety chair flash by, and fade. And then I am back, back in this country not of my birth, and it claims me, just like that, without even saying, "May I?" Little by little, I forget the *Siciliana* I was a couple of weeks ago, and the familiar ache returns, sits right in the middle of my chest. It owns me. My throat tightens, and English words crawl out of me — stiff, unreal, foreign, these spiteful pretenders.

When We First Arrived, 1983

Gabriela Halas

Poetry

NATIONALITY Czech
FIRST LANGUAGE Czech
SECOND LANGUAGE English

Appeared in Issue Spring '21

America opened —
Prairies unfolded in ever-arriving
distance. Air untarnished, fresh.

Our eyes followed waves of power lines,
their undulating surge of promise.
Impenetrable words

crowded the air
like dense boreal. We needed to split the tongue,
slit like seismic lines;

corridors of language connected,
fragmented. Government placement
in small-town Alberta. *Ameri-ka,*

Kanada — an immigrant knows
how to replace one
for the other. Old words ruptured —

new ones formed like plaster
around our mouths.
We drove north

When We First Arrived, 1983

where my father, with his six-month-old English,
found work in oil-rich mines.
Bowls of earth carved

like a god's terraced garden. Drunken spruce sank
in sedated chaos
like our immigrant thoughts —

where nothing is as it appears.
I remember taking my thumb and forefinger,
traversing an atlas; stretched to shape

our tiny country resting along the buckled spine
of the Rockies, hardly filling an eighth
of this new place. Nearly treeless lawns, in awe —

the gentle slow arc of water,
watering. Every house had a spare room
or three. Fenced front and back,

our own private country's small walls
stood in perfect symmetry.
Our father spent twenty years

in shift-work at the machine shop; an informal United
Nations. Our mother, a lifetime cashier,
her daughters the first to go to school.

Nearly forty years later,
the newly arrived,
as we once were,

find fences,
straight,
are not flush; weighted

Gabriela Halas

like walls. They are meant
to be climbed.
Threats shouted in *America*,

Canada — twists of the tongue.
Words crowd the air
like rush-hour traffic.

We are all born somewhere
we do not end up.

History Flooding the Continent
Ioana Morpurgo

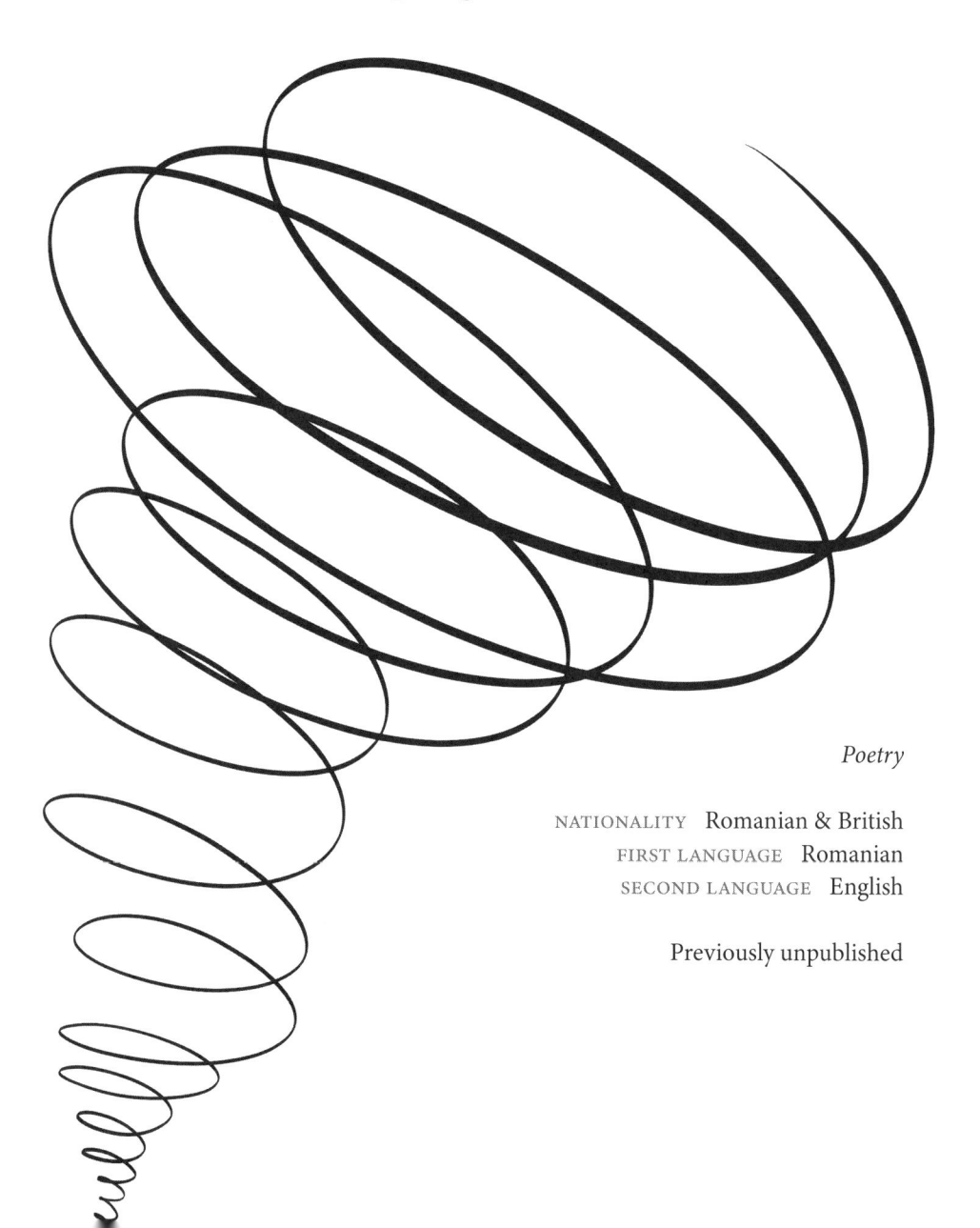

Poetry

NATIONALITY Romanian & British
FIRST LANGUAGE Romanian
SECOND LANGUAGE English

Previously unpublished

And so she sets off
the length of human episteme
Crop upon mass grave upon new crop
adulterating the history of species
with a flap of a razor blade wing
she dives grenade-style into
lovers' isolated dreams to bring them together
by mortar
        for all the vortexes of memory
        she brings respite
        for all disseminated yet muted semen
        she sets up direct debit
        for lullabies
Convergent allegories run riot
yet time fosters every child of living emotion
offering solace as logos praxis rhyme
She bites time
        Danube Dnipro Vistula Prut
        some wrote down hate
        some slept
        some recited
From those vortexes of memory
unlikely floating devices make it to the shore
asylum is a gleaming silky thing no weight no fright no engine
some pasts make it
some don't
Her shadow hovers razor blade intact
splitting tear from eye and eye from vision
immaculate division
and here I crouch to the ground and whisper to such roots
as available
Wait wait for eternity
She shall be donating blood
Soon.

Immigrant Sitcom
Francisco Serrano

Flash Nonfiction

NATIONALITY Mexican
FIRST LANGUAGE Spanish
SECOND LANGUAGE English

Appeared in Issue Spring '20

When you are an immigrant on the cusp of being American, meaning you came to America early enough you end up knowing more about *here* than *there* but late enough that the government treats you differently than your classmates, you come to realize your issues and theirs are not the same. Not getting asked to the homecoming dance is not as scary as your family being gone when you come home the day of the homecoming dance.

And if you knew me, you would be asking me, "Why are you worrying so much? You're not a criminal… and your family is so nice all the time." American naiveness; still thinking people in uniforms would notice or care about the difference.

In a time where television shapes your outlook, I wish there was a TV sitcom about immigrants; a coming-of-age TV sitcom episode where the 15-year-old learns they cannot get a license or a job or travel abroad after taking French at school and planning their trip with their friends. How will they deal with it? Stay tuned for the next episode!

Or like a Mother's Day episode where a Latina woman is asking her 6-year-old son what kind of snacks he wants and suddenly a white woman approaches her with foam in her mouth, screaming at her,

"GO BACK TO YOUR COUNTRY."

"NOBODY WANTS YOU HERE."

"SPEAK ENGLISH."

Then it cuts to the mother putting her child to sleep by giving them a kiss on the forehead, walking to the kitchen and then silently crying under the one single lightbulb. Maybe then America will not look away and finally say "awww," along with the live studio audience. Or maybe a lighter take on the immigrant experience, like when 14-year-old Brenda starts working in the same factory her mom works in during the summer instead of taking the sun by the pool. But it's not so bad, because during lunchtime she sits with the other underage kids working under illegal names. Maybe the audience will want to rewatch them over and over and over like they do with *Friends*. Maybe it would even be on Disney! Then our children would be children. Not baggage, not dirty criminals, not drug dealers. Since people are so tired of the news because it makes them so sad, I think going with a Disney vibe would be so refreshing, right?

Maybe we'll get more than one season. In season 2, maybe the main character deals with not being an all straight-A student or valedictorian but still feels like he matters to this country... right? In season 3, the immigrant parents go to therapy and heal all the hurt they have inside. In season 4, if we get confirmed for it, it would be cool to see the immigrant protagonist cry from happiness for once. Not out of relief because the worst didn't happen: just pure joy, could be a great plot twist. I think we should see immigrant experiences on a TV screen with lines and plots for people to understand that we are robbing generations of their childhood. How will kids deal with normal teenager problems when they're seeing moms, dads, daughters, sons, and neighbors like theirs being mistreated, being abused, tormented and separated, without warning; without pity? A theme song will play where a nearly bald white man in a classic dark blue suit cuts the umbilical cord and throws it across the border and says, "go fetch."

The Singing Tree
Nilofar Shidmehr

Fiction

NATIONALITY Iranian & Canadian
FIRST LANGUAGE Persian
SECOND LANGUAGE English

Previously unpublished

When I first saw the oak across the street — parched, neglected, barely surviving — it made me want to cry. Like me it was withering, with only one major branch remaining, clinging to life, just barely. Rather than help I kept my curtains closed. I didn't want to be reminded of what lay ahead for that tree, and for me.

In my country, they say you forget people and things — even your loved ones — if you don't see them. And that's exactly what happened with that oak: For a long time, I forgot that it existed.

I am a middle-aged, first-generation immigrant. I don't have children and I live on the outskirts of a metropole in a bachelor suite which I own.

When I first saw the oak, I had a job as a security guard at the Museum of Modern Art. Given my language deficiencies, this was the only work I could get. It was always the same routine: After a solitary breakfast, I'd spend most of my day at the museum, then finish with a sad dinner alone. At work I was just as lonely as I was at home, standing in a corner of an exhibition room watching visitors who were interested in objects on display — not in me. They usually walked by without noticing my presence. I wasn't a point of reference except for when someone was looking for the restroom or was lost and couldn't find their way out.

In the beginning I liked my job because it allowed me to remain mute. I had noticed that in this new country, people were not often forgiving of difference. *Who wanted to be identified by her "funny" accent or her "awkward and strange" pronunciation? Not me!*

Coming home from work, exhausted, I spent most evenings watching TV. I sprawled on the sofa observing characters moving across the screen. Like the exhibition crowd, they were oblivious to my existence. From time to time, when my eyes started aching from staring at the screen, I glanced around my sparsely furnished room, looking at the walls which confined me. At the museum, when I became tired of people, I could escape by leaning back, resting my head against a wall and dozing. I had a chance to interact with others this way, if only in my dreams. There, I had in-depth conversations in my mother tongue — conversations that went far beyond the typical exchanges I had at work. These consisted of a few rudimentary words, spoken quietly so that I wouldn't be recognized as "different." Words such as: *Hi, Bye, Thanks, Yes, No.* But then I started losing sleep, at work and at home, missing a chance to speak even to a figment of my imagination. Then I experienced an agonizing worry. *What if I lose my language, since I don't use it?*

That's when I decided to speak — in my mind — to the paintings and statues at the museum. And I'd speak at home, to my bed, chair, and table. I even talked to the TV which I always kept on. Since media personalities rarely went silent, I spoke over them. After a while, however, I'd run out of words while they jabbered on and on. Listening to them, with closed eyes, exhaustion would swallow me and I'd fall into a dreamless sleep. Shortly after, I'd wake up, drenched in sweat, with a pounding heart, finding myself in darkness. The only available light came from the TV, which was still talking gibberish. I'd turn away toward the wall against which my bed rested. But that was not enough to ease the hard feeling of alienation rising within me. Unintelligible words echoed off the walls and drowned me in estrangement. Mustering every ounce of energy in my limbs, I'd climb out of bed, dress and leave to roam empty streets until dawn.

Sometimes I didn't come home for breakfast and went straight to work. To kill time, I tramped along avenues or sat at coffeeshops by myself, listening to locals' conversations. Unfortunately, that didn't make me more fluent in the language they were speaking.

Every night, I travelled further from my place. It took me all night to march back home. Usually, when I reached my building, it was just before dawn. Every window was dark, but mine flickered with the television's light.

There were occasions when my swollen feet could barely haul my dog-tired body up the stairs, all the way to the door of my bachelor suite. But then my hands wouldn't collaborate — wouldn't pull my keys from my purse, grab the knob, and turn it open. I'd go outside again — breathless.

When I did open the door and let myself in, I'd undress and pass the TV with eyes averted and drop myself onto the bed. I'd wake up to a bright room, fumble for the clothes I'd left on the floor, and immediately leave for work. The fridge was almost empty and, in most cases, I was too tired to have even my solitary breakfast.

This routine was unsustainable. I needed to rest, otherwise I'd lose my job. And loneliness hurt more than my exhaustion or the pain in my legs. It gnawed at my soul. That's why I advertised for a roommate in a community newspaper.

A steady stream of roommates followed. All of them were refugees or new immigrants. Each would leave after a short while, once they found out my language abilities were no better than theirs. Had they stayed, they all said, they would never settle down, find a good job or progress in life. And they were right: They didn't come to this new country to speak and practice their own language with an expatriate. But that was exactly the reason I brought them in. I didn't wish to translate my thoughts into another language. Translations created misunderstandings which I aimed to avoid.

My roommates often didn't talk to me on weekends. A few times, when we had deep conversations, they turned into heated debates about politics. Small talk was rare and boring, ending in long and strenuous arguments over trivial things like weekly chores. Our worst fights were over the TV which I insisted be kept on all the time. To ease conflict, I often went back home only after my roommates were sleeping. On weekdays, I'd leave home before they were up. Again, exhaustion and a feeling of estrangement took their toll on me.

My last roommate hurt me in an unexpected way. He moved out in my absence and took the TV with him. I was traumatized at first, but then settled back into my solitary life. It wasn't that bad, after all, without television. The room's quiet allowed me to sleep and recover my health. I even felt content to be left alone, enjoying for the first time the silence of my residence.

Alas, it didn't last long. Loneliness returned in waves. And, more than my disagreeable roommates, I missed the background blathering of the TV. I wished I could still talk to — or talk over — the television's characters. I won all arguments with them. I had the power to mute them the same way I had been rendered mute so many times, when people pretended they didn't understand me or understood very little. Sometimes, because of my differences, I couldn't help but feel stupid, so I kept my mouth shut. The TV characters were all friendly. None of them ever turned hostile. Since they couldn't hear me, they didn't mind my strange tongue. There were no misunderstandings and no apologies necessary.

Loneliness kept me awake at night. I couldn't bear the pressure that the four surrounding walls seemed to exert on me. I thought it must be similar to the pressure a dead person feels on the first night in her grave. But what could I do? I was fed up with staying out in the street and I couldn't bear just lying in bed, staring at the ceiling all night and waiting for the morning. All I could do was to pray for a miracle to turn me into a person, like ordinary people in this country. What if I became a replica — a doll speaking proper language when a button is pushed, hidden on her back, under her clothing?

Haunted by that image every night, I prayed for agreeable company, someone who would speak a language I knew. Someone who didn't wish to assimilate and would listen to me when I spoke as my ancestors did. Since I don't believe in any established religion, I prayed to my own "God of Mother Tongues."

To my surprise, praying worked. One night, coming back from work, I noticed my curtains drawn back and the window lit from inside. I hurried up to my apartment. The door was ajar. I pushed it fully open and stepped in, eager to see who my uninvited guest might be. I looked around, dazzled by an unusual brightness in the room. As my eyes became accustomed to the light, I noticed someone lounging on the couch. My mouth dropped open in amazement: She was a woman of color, a woman who looked exactly like me!

She was looking out the window at the tree across the street. The oak I'd forgotten about a long time ago was still there. The last time I had seen it, the tree had had only one branch. But today, I noted two. And even from a distance, I could see leaves starting to bud. I smiled and turned to the stranger in my room. She seemed so relaxed, as if my home was also hers. I didn't want to disturb her but I couldn't stay silent. *Who are you?* I asked.

She turned from the tree toward me, gave a heartfelt smile, and answered in a language I didn't understand but which was soothing, like a lullaby. I sat next to her, feeling her calmness seep into my body and put me at ease. Her understanding face prompted me to talk about what burdened my heart — the exodus of my people and the trials and tribulations I had faced since landing in this country. She nodded in an agreeable manner. It was amazing to talk so freely, to feel so comfortable with this stranger. I could finally speak of my long-lived loneliness and suffering. Apparently, I hadn't lost my language. I was as fluent as I was in my motherland.

She spoke again and I listened. Only then did I realize that she projected joy. She radiated the goodwill of an expectant mother. I pointed to her belly and raised my eyebrows. She nodded and flashed a heartwarming and exuberant smile. That night we slept together on my bed, facing one another like twins — with my hand resting on her belly. In the morning, I woke from the most colorful sleep of my life and prepared breakfast for two.

After work, I rushed back home to make dinner for us. I soared up the staircase and sauntered into my apartment to be with her as soon as possible. This time, my room's brightness seemed to have doubled. My eyes were fully open but I couldn't believe them. Next to my new roommate sat a girl — a replica of me when I was younger. Stepping closer to this new guest, the same questions I'd asked the day before jumped to mind: *Who are you? What's your name?*

In response, she emanated the same encouraging expression that helped me understand that the older woman was pregnant.

Over dinner, I recounted the events of my day to them. They listened attentively, but strangely, from time to time, their heads would turn toward the tree across the street. During these moments, they would nod and softly murmur "mm-h," indicating their understanding. They even laughed when I told a joke. Later I listened to their stories — tales expressed in two distinct languages. I was sure my roommates' mother tongues were different. Did they understand each other? I wasn't sure, but I realized I was beginning to understand them both. Whenever I directed my attention toward the tree, a new level of comprehension dawned on me.

During our conversations, the oak grew more branches. Birds nested in the fresh greenery and sang. They resembled us, with our different languages. I was sure they would come to know each other's songs by heart. Magically, those tunes mingled, creating a magnificent symphony. And that oak became a singing tree.

As the evening dwindled and the light outside dimmed, my companions and I moved to the bed and lay down. The pregnant girl on her back and the other two of us on our sides, facing her, fingers interwoven across her belly.

Over time, we multiplied but lived peacefully with one another in my place. I no longer felt confined or lonely. I abandoned my plan to move back to my motherland. Here, I lived among strange visitors I considered my kin. My room transformed into our permanent residence, its walls echoing happy tunes like a song box.

We kept the curtains pulled back and the window open to enjoy the green face of our inspiration — the thriving oak across the street. I slept deep and content and no longer felt an urge to run or stay out in the streets.

Since then, until now, I've been well-rooted and secure. I am branching out with many selves who speak the languages of the world. I sing every day.

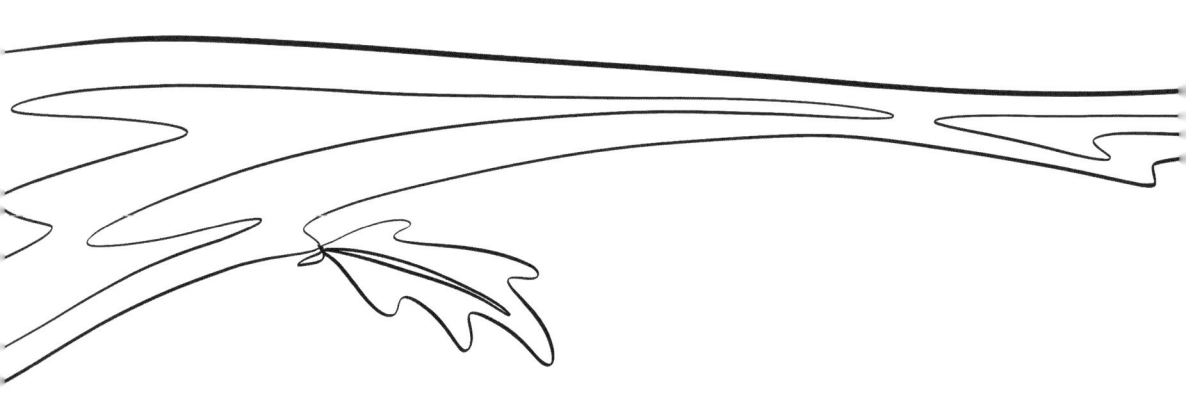

UPHEAVAL

Traumatic experiences and their aftermaths can take many shapes. They can hit us as singular events, or fall upon us as a continuous oppression by toxic social systems or harmful cultural ideologies; they can be immediately felt as shocks, or go unrecognized at first only to return and haunt us in later life;[11] and they can be an intimately personal experience, a collective tragedy, or both at once.[12] Taking into account the various causes of traumas and their extension across generations, the sheer magnitude of potential and experienced upheaval on our planet every day can be overwhelming — to put it mildly.

Literature gives us a place to process, voice and grasp this intangible multiplicity of disturbing situations. Writers can find healing in creative narratives or poems which allow them to "reclaim [their] most painful experiences,"[13] while readers and writers alike are given the chance to imagine themselves in the bodies and minds of their fellow human beings and reflect on what it is that leads to these experiences in the first place.

The literary texts in this section approach the theme of trauma from various angles. Loss, abuse, fear, war, persecution and mistreatment are among the themes represented in this collection of texts by ESL writers, intertwined and put into perspective by the individual entries. Some are fictional, some memoir pieces, and some poetic expressions of what memory reveals and imagination adds.[14] Some seem place- and timeless, out-of-one's-own-body, and almost unreal, others appear deeply rooted in our shared history, dive into one's innermost fabrics and are just too real in all their density and focus.

There is no handbook to an uprooting of one's life and the following struggle of coming to terms with it. Every individual lives through the transformation from a self before to a self after the traumatic experience in their unique way. Meaning and value are reconstructed, a new reality with new knowledge is established, and the laws and social norms of our environments are reevaluated.[15] The following texts are a testament to the benefits of looking at this process from a cross-cultural perspective. They will allow you to get under the skin of fictionalized individuals from various regions on this earth, coming together in the English language, which represents in the case of second language writers a further transformation — namely one on the linguistic level.

by Lisa Schantl

Hard Labor: Childbirth Soviet Style

Galina Chernaya

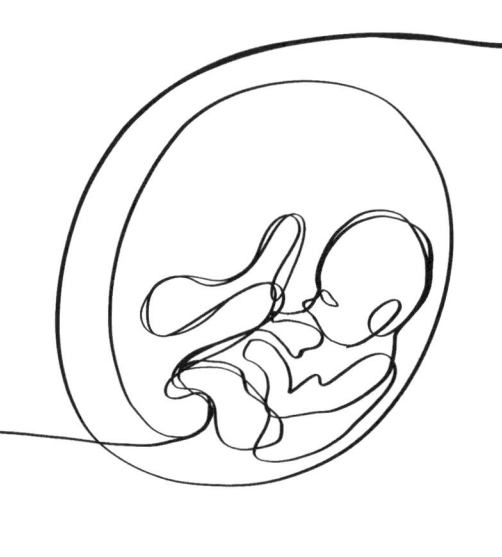

Nonfiction

NATIONALITY U.S.
FIRST LANGUAGE Russian
SECOND LANGUAGE English

Appeared in Issue Fall '23

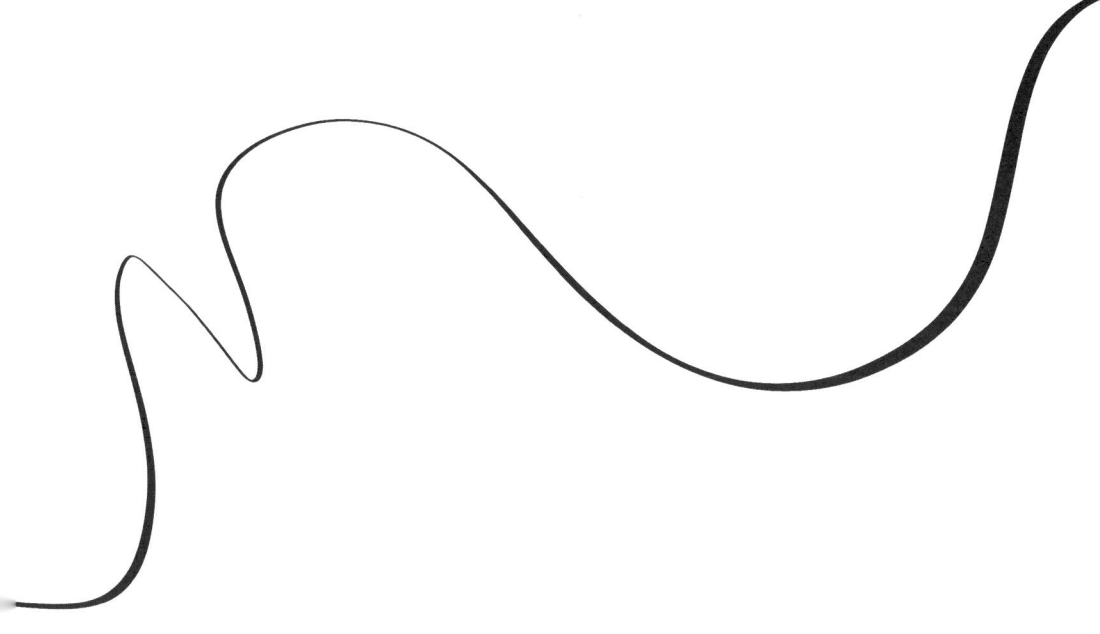

> Why do people always say you forget the pain of labor? I haven't forgotten the pain of labor. Labor hurt. It hurt a lot. The fact that I am not currently in pain and cannot simulate the pain of labor doesn't mean I don't remember it.
> — Nora Ephron, *O, The Oprah Magazine,* October 2005

As it is for most mothers, I remember the day I gave birth to each of my children as one of the most memorable days of my life, but even now, forty years later, the trauma of birth of my first child still stands out as an extremely vivid, hyper-realistic experience. Like most pregnancies in the Soviet Union, this one was unplanned. When I learned I was pregnant in May 1981, I was a 21-year-old student in a Master's degree program at Moscow University, from which I was due to graduate the following year in June. Abortions were legal and very common, but I did not consider this option. To avoid rumors of infertility, a married woman was expected to have a baby within the first three years of marriage, and my three years were already up.

I kept my pregnancy private, as was customary, and managed to go unnoticed until I was seven months along. It was already winter and finals were scheduled through the entire month of January, the last one being just a week before my February 6 due date. Like others in my situation, I was allowed to take the exams ahead of schedule. I passed my last one on January 13.

As if my baby knew exams were over, she woke up kicking on January 14. My first symptom of what was to come was severe back pain. There was no *What to Expect When You're Expecting* or any other books about pregnancy in the Soviet Union and childbirth classes were unheard of. This meant that first-time mothers could only learn about pregnancy and labor from older women willing to share their experiences. My mother didn't tell me much, except that giving birth to me, the youngest of her three children, was the hardest. "When your water breaks, you call emergency services," was her only advice.

This is what I absolutely did *not* want to do. I knew that if I called 03 (the Soviet 911), I would be taken to any delivery hospital with an available bed. Delivery hospitals were separate entities from regular hospitals, and I could end up anywhere in Moscow. Even more importantly, the vast majority of Moscow delivery hospitals were hotbeds of staph infection, and there was no guarantee that the hospital I ended up in would be safe.

Lucky for me, my mother-in-law was a leading obstetrician-gynecologist at the U. S. S. R. Ministry of Health. She had arranged for me to give birth at the Ministry's Institute of Obstetrics and Gynecology, which had the best obstetricians in the country and was known to be staph-free. "It's considered a bad sign if a doctor delivers a relative's baby, so I will not be with you in the delivery room," she advised. However, as a Department Chair at the Institute, she had full trust in her colleagues. "Don't worry," she assured me. "You'll be in good hands."

My contractions started in the early afternoon. At first, they were just uncomfortable, not painful. I was home by myself, but I didn't call anyone because my water didn't break. By the time my husband Kostya got home from work around 5 p.m., I was in real pain. Fortunately, the Institute of Obstetrics and Gynecology was only a ten-minute walk from the apartment. We left right away, taking nothing for me or the baby — due to fear of infection, no personal items or anything else from the outside were permitted in Soviet maternity wards.

The weather was brutally cold. I walked very slowly, hobbling with Kostya's help from one street light to the next, stopping under each to take a deep gulp of air. The contractions were still slow, but more insistent now. I remember grabbing a lamppost, hard, and drawing in a sharp breath. The air was muffled and warm, and smelled of damp wool through the scarf wound protectively over my lower face.

At the hospital, the clock in the waiting area showed 6:05 p.m. We were taken to an examination room where I was checked for dilation and admitted. From this point on, it was all uncharted territory: No family members were allowed during labor or delivery. I took off my wedding ring and handed it to Kostya — jewelry was not permitted — and kissed him goodbye.

As expected, I was told to change into a patient gown and a nurse accompanied me to a labor prep room. Not expected was the next step, when a different nurse shaved off all my pubic hair with a single-edged razor. She made no effort to hide her disgust, and even managed to make a few nicks, which immediately started itching. Then came the enema to clear my bowels, and I was ready for the labor room.

Walking in, I was hit by the blinding glare of fluorescent ceiling lamps bouncing off the white-tiled walls. Totally white and antiseptic, the room shone from floor to ceiling with brilliantly reflected light. Two female nurses in uniforms and scrub caps moved among a dozen or so hospital beds, filled with women in various stages of labor all lined up in neat rows. The windows along the outer wall were also painted white to prohibit any prying exterior gaze from penetrating the room.

I was pointed to one of the few free beds in a corner. It was metal, with a thin, pallet-like mattress sheathed in pale oilcloth. I lay down — no sitting or walking permitted — and looked around with a feeling of mounting panic. Most women were moaning. One or two were in advanced labor, letting out terrible screams with every contraction. My immediate neighbor was crying, constantly calling her husband's name: "Vasya, Vasya, what did you do to me?" she kept groaning over and over.

Two midwives on their hourly rounds moved routinely among the rows, checking dilation to determine who was ready for delivery. "Keep it up, woman! Yell! Scream so hard your voice gives out!" was their only encouragement. Every birth was natural — there was no pain management in maternity wards, and epidurals were a thing unknown. Being only 21, I was emotionally unprepared to witness, let alone experience, such suffering.

My labor progressed, the pain became more intense, and I entered the realm of the screamers. After a few hours, I could not remember where I was or why. I was one with the excruciating pain, and all I wanted was for that pain to end. As I learned later, not everything was going well. My baby was suffering from asynclitic presentation — her head was tilted to one side, and she was unable to move down the birth canal in spite of intense contractions. The next eight hours melded together in delirium — echoing shrieks, the clock stopped dead on the wall, sweat streaming down my forehead, my teeth chattering from the cold.

By 6 a.m., my baby was in extreme distress and my contractions had slowed. Unable to think of a better option, the doctor decided to stimulate contraction, and administered an intravenous drug. The contractions intensified until the pain became so unbearable that I tried to yank the IV out of my arm. Nurses roughly grabbed my hands, and I managed to bite one on the forearm. They tied me down and shoved an oxygen mask over my nose and mouth.

Fighting to escape, I heard the doctor mention "C-section." Very rare in the Soviet Union, the procedure was reserved as a last resort in complex, life-threatening cases. "Let's try one last thing," a nurse said. "Call Andrusha."

A huge male nurse suddenly appeared. He knew exactly what he'd been called in to do, and exactly how to do it. And lucky for me and my baby that he did — for his job was to perform the Kristeller Maneuver, or "fundal push," a harrowing, high-risk procedure that carries the threat of uterine rupture and infant brain damage.

Looming over me, he placed the flat of his big palms on my stomach, bent over and, with all his strength, pressed the entire weight of his upper body down against my belly. I screamed at the top of my lungs, feeling as if every vessel in my body had burst at once.

But it worked! Tearing everything on her way, my baby daughter finally ripped her way out at 8:20 a.m. A nurse lifted her in the air to show her to me. Poor baby! Her head was one big, purple bruise, with a groove on the left side from banging for hours against my pelvis. The nurse whisked her away without letting me hold her. This was protocol: Babies were always separated from their mothers at birth. A few minutes later, the same nurse came back to give me the statistics: My baby girl weighed 6 pounds and 6 ounces, and was 19 ½ inches long (3 kg, 50 cm). Her oxygen level was a bit low, but otherwise she was healthy. I was flooded with relief.

But it was not over for me yet. I was badly torn and had to be sutured. Again, no anesthesia of any kind was used. Writhing in pain, I asked the midwife stitching me up how much longer it would take. "It's over when I'm done," she barked. When she finally tied the last knot, I was not wheeled into the recovery room but was left uncovered on a gurney by a drafty window in the corridor and forbidden to sleep for two hours. A nurse came by every fifteen minutes to keep me awake and check I hadn't died of internal bleeding or other complications. "Woman, no sleeping!" she growled, whenever I closed my eyes.

Around 9 a.m., it started to lighten up outside. The sky above the surrounding buildings was turning deep red, the color of the stains on my gown. It was mid-January, the coldest time of the year in Moscow, when daytime temperatures rarely rise above −20 °C (−4 °F). A red sunrise signaled an exceptionally cold day ahead. And indeed, January 15, 1982, the day my wonderful daughter came into this world, was bone-chilling cold.

After the obligatory two hours in the hallway, my arms and legs numb from the cold, I was transferred to the maternity floor. I was the last new mother to be placed in the room. Most occupants were women I'd seen in the labor room. All ten of us had given birth the same night. At last, I could sleep.

When I woke up, I crawled out of bed and stumbled to the sink at the front of the room. One look in the mirror, and tears started coming down my cheeks. I didn't recognize my own face — eyes red with burst capillaries, face bruised and heavily marked from the oxygen mask, tangled hair, oily from sweat, clotted with dried blood. The sutures made it so painful to walk, I barely made it back to bed.

There was no toilet in the room, and walking down the corridor to the bathroom, an endeavor in itself, was even more difficult because I had no underwear. In the firm belief that airing stitches promoted healing, no underwear was permitted in the hospital. Instead, women were given two pieces of cloth a day to absorb vaginal discharge. Walking required taking tiny steps while tightly squeezing the cloth between my legs. *Like Japanese women walking in kimonos*, I thought as I tottered down the hall, though our ugly, bleached hospital gowns were certainly no match for beautiful Japanese silk robes.

> In the movies where people have babies, they are sitting in a hospital bed with flowers everywhere, beautifully made-up, with a baby in their arms and it is all very lovely. Anyone who has been in that zone will know it's total fiction. It's a truly, truly murderous business. Giving birth is a violent thing to go through.
> —Tilda Swinton, *Marie Claire*, May 2011

Since neither the mother nor the baby endured permanent damage, my delivery was considered perfectly normal. Even so, hospital rules required a minimum one-week stay in the maternity ward, during which no visitors were allowed. The only way fathers could "visit" their wives and newborns was to stand outside the tightly sealed, winterized windows, and hope to hear a few words through the glass. I asked Kostya not to come, but the woman in the next bed, who turned out to have been next to me during labor as well, wanted to see her husband daily.

Yana was 18 and a newlywed. Her husband, Vasya, also 18, showed up by the window several times a day. Most of the time he was drunk — he'd been celebrating the arrival of his baby daughter since the day Yana gave birth. "These stitches really hurt!" Yana complained, shouting through the window. "They didn't sew up your hole, did they?" Vasya yelled back through the glass. Everyone in the room giggled.

All newborns were swaddled and kept together in a single room away from their mothers — again, from fear of infection. A two-factor identification system was used to avoid confusion: Immediately after birth, the mother's name, baby's gender, and delivery date were hand-written on two small squares of oilcloth. One tag was tied around the newborn's wrist, and the other was attached to the baby's swaddling clothes. The ID needed to be removed and reattached every time a baby was changed — a minimum of six times a day — so human error was intrinsic to the system. I witnessed this myself in the hospital when I encountered a sobbing woman with a newborn in her arms who'd returned to report her baby's name tags didn't match. "Can't you tell if it's your own baby?" asked the administrator, clearly annoyed by her tears. "No!" she cried. "They all look alike to me!"

Every four hours, babies were routinely rolled in carts from the nursery to their mothers' room for nursing. The carts were large enough to transport ten to twelve swaddled infants, tightly packed side to side. I would soon be starting my PhD program, so I decided not to nurse Katya. This was very rare in the Soviet Union. With the help of my mother-in-law, I was able to buy Parlodel pills, a foreign-made medication to suppress lactation, and a foreign formula, Similac, both unavailable in pharmacies.

Katya was bottle-fed by the nurses, so I was only permitted to hold her once a day. How eagerly I waited for the nurse to bring her in! While the other mothers nursed, I held Katya in my arms, cherishing every one of the few moments I was allowed to spend with her. As she was tightly swaddled, I couldn't see her body, but I loved smiling down at her tiny face, grimacing and blowing air bubbles. She never cried, not even once. To me she was simply beautiful.

Except for precious moments with Katya, I was soon bored out of my mind. There was no TV or radio, so women spent the days talking about their deliveries, their husbands, and their other kids. At age 21, I fell in the middle of the pack: Four women were older than me (that is to say, in their twenties), and four were still teenagers. The single outlier was 36, and had just given birth to her third child. To give birth in your mid-thirties was all but unheard of for a Soviet woman. The only exception I was aware of was my mother, who had given birth to me at age 35, after her second child, my sister Olga, had died of childhood leukemia at age 2. My whole life, my parents kept reminding me that I was a replacement for my middle sister.

We were astounded to learn that the oldest woman was a foreigner. Helen was English, her husband was on the British embassy staff, and their family of four had been living in Moscow for five years. Due to her age, we readily nicknamed her "Babushka." She was not offended and went along with the joke.

Helen's Russian was very good, but when I offered to speak English in hope of practicing my language skills, she happily agreed. My first question was why she had chosen to give birth in Moscow instead of England. "Both my children were born in London, so I wanted to have a different experience," she explained. "It worked out fine: My labor was short and I had an easy delivery." What she didn't say was that she'd received special treatment as a foreigner: Her husband was allowed to see her in the Director's Office. He once brought the nurses a big box of Earl Grey tea bags, and Helen kindly asked a nurse to make me a cup. It was so good. That slightly bitter smell of bergamot was literally and metaphorically from another world!

January 22 came at last, and Katya and I were released from the hospital. Kostya was waiting in the discharge room. We hugged, and I changed into the clothes he'd brought while a nurse I'd never seen before went to get Katya. "It's freezing outside. Did you bring enough blankets for Katya?" I asked. "Yes, and my father's here to drive us home."

Just then, the door opened and the nurse entered with Katya. In keeping with long-standing tradition, she handed the baby to her father: "Here you go, Daddy," she said, turning sidewise so Kostya could stick money in her pocket — another long-standing tradition. This obligatory "tip" — which was more of a "service fee" for handing over a baby to its father — was well-defined: 15 to 20 rubles for a girl, and 25 to 30 for a boy. For the sake of comparison, I add that Kostya, a 25-year-old junior researcher at the Physics Institute of the Academy of Sciences, earned 140 rubles a month.

Handling Katya as I would a crystal vase, I wrapped her in both of the blankets Kostya had brought, and we stepped outside. After being locked up for a week, inhaling the fresh cold air felt wonderfully invigorating. Kostya's father met us by the door. "Where's that little beauty queen?" he asked with a smile, trying to peep under the blanket protecting Katya's face. "No, no, please wait until we get home," I begged. "The air's far too cold for the baby."

Riding home in the car, I thought about how my mother had spent two whole days on the phone bragging about her first grandchild, my older sister's daughter. "Natasha did a wonderful job! The baby is picture-perfect — and a healthy size too, 7½ pounds. Her skin is flawless! Oh! And you should see her plump little cheeks, so full and round when she's nursing! Natasha's going to be an amazing mother!"

What will she say about Katya and me? was all I could think. Katya could not measure up to her cousin's perfection, and my mother had made it abundantly clear that she highly disapproved of my decision not to nurse. Had she already judged me as a bad mother?

No sooner were we home than my mother arrived. I was so anxious for her admiration that my heart started pounding the minute she walked in the door. I unswaddled Katya for her inspection. She looked much better but had lost some weight and was now at 6 pounds. My mother took one glance and gave a little chuckle. "*Hmmm!* I have never seen such a puny baby. And, as you know, today is your father's birthday. I have to go right away. Some of his colleagues are coming for dinner, and I've got to prepare." And with that, she left. Expecting worse, I felt relieved.

An hour later, Kostya and his father also returned to work, leaving me with my newborn daughter quietly sleeping in her crib. It was the first time we'd ever been alone together. I listened to her peacefully breathing, my mind swirling with worry. *What do I do when she cries? What if she screams and I can't calm her down? Will she take her formula? What if she chokes?*

I soon discovered that caring for an infant took a whole lot of time and work. In my day, for example, babies were still traditionally swaddled because it was thought they felt more secure snuggly wrapped in a blanket. I mastered the technique in a couple of days, but keeping the baby clean was another matter. Traditional flannel receiving blankets, just like those in the States, were used for swaddling. At the very minimum, they had to be changed before every feeding and after every bowel movement. This added up to a good ten soiled blankets, all to be washed at the end of the day.

To make matters worse, commercially made disposable diapers were not yet available in the Soviet Union. We made them ourselves the old-fashioned way, folding cheesecloth eight to ten times over and stitching the layers together by hand. Like most families, we had no washing machine, so every night I hand-washed all the diapers and blankets, wrung them out, and hung them to dry on a line strung up in the kitchen.

All in all, I was fortunate. Katya was an easy baby and we soon established a routine. Though not always willing to eat at designated times, she was a good sleeper. January quickly came to an end, and Kostya took four weeks off in February, the maximum leave allowed for the year, to stay home with the baby so I could return to school. On February 7, the first day of spring semester, I was back in class. By then, I was almost at my pre-pregnancy weight. "Galya, you don't look like someone who just had a baby three weeks ago!" exclaimed one of my classmates. "How did you do it? Did you just spit it out?"

"It wasn't quite like spitting," I replied. "But it was fine."

Public discussion of obstetric abuse is still muzzled in Russia and many other countries, notably including the United States. For stories of surviving and witnessing such cases, see Birth Monopoly's "Obstetric Violence Stories Map," the first worldwide, public database of abusive maternity care stories.

Snake Baby

Min "Matthew" Choi

Fiction

NATIONALITY Korean & American
FIRST LANGUAGE Korean
SECOND LANGUAGE English

Appeared in Issue Fall '22

Snake baby came to me in a neat glass bottle, corked at the top with cellophane wrapped around it all. Mama bought it from abroad two years ago, slid it onto my table, said if you're gonna drink, drink that instead. Snake wine: medicinal, reckless, another bottle that teased the nose like vinegar, reptile essence infused into the liquor, venom molecularly deconstructed by the ethanol and turned into spiritual pharmaceutics. It's perfectly safe, it's good for you, she assured me.

But the world folds up in landscape, creases over my mother in less than a year, draws color out of her nails, her teeth. Hair gray, coffin brown, nothing to see except empty aisles when I arrive, clutching my skin together with a safety pin.

Snake baby was supposed to be dead, a cherry heart choked up, ingrained in grain. That's all it was at first, just the heart soaked in spice, but when I empty the bottle, it sours my tongue, embitters me as it washes down, numbness injects into my feet as I climb up the stairs, step after step. I lay down in my bed after — it's all I can manage after the funeral — and as unconsciousness kidnaps me, another heart beats with mine, two imprints above the bedsheets, a life inside my own. I cry and cry and my pillow goes cold against my ear; I am turned into a stone to be skipped over mild waters. I dream that I am liquid in a bottle, that I am shapeless, that I hold inside me anything at all.

The next morning brings motion. Snake baby isn't afraid to kick, flex its dorsal fins around concrete bone, slide slick in between my rib cage and pantomime compressions. When I stare at myself in the mirror, I can't see it. I know it's filling in the empty space between my organs but my body looks as it always has: skinny, 5-foot-10, arms thinning to bone with not a trace of snake. I close my eyes and I envision my entrails. The pattern of scales imprinted in blood, a plasma-coated serpent circumnavigating my body. Closing my eyes tighter, I turn off the lights and let the fan go quiet. Wind cuts my body, traces out Snake baby's figure in the darkness, and I press my hand against my right thigh, where the muscle pulls itself taut in serpentine fashion. Its shape materializes in my palms and I trace it down to my knee, reading the curved vertebrae like braille.

I speak to it: *You're a snake baby living inside me.*

It responds in combat. Snake baby whips its tail in the narrow space and it strikes twice, the windup and the snap both scald against muscle. It stings from the inside, my thigh knots up in pain and I keel over. Inhale. Exhale, let my vision clear. My leg loosens, aftershocks starting from quads and moving over my calves, tensing at the shins. Snake baby wraps around my shin, and walks me into the shower, heaving one paralyzed foot then the next. *Oh children*, I think. Snake baby likes the steam. Cozies up in the heat. To its disappointment, I regain control, lift myself up and out of the steam. *I gotta get to work, my sweet Snake baby.* It hangs off my collarbone, momentarily satisfied by the steam.

I'm halfway between my car and the office when I trip. I try to gather my balance, swing myself upright, but it jostles Snake baby, and it bites me from the inside. Should've called in sick to work, told the boss I was aching all over, but I never do. Once the fangs sink in, it takes just a few seconds, then I can't tell the difference between my left foot and my right hand or my right eye from the crack of my ass and everything gets tripped up like a shoelace tied all wrong, three bunny ears crisscrossed instead of two. I fall to my side and my head cracks open against the concrete. Something warm trails out from the open wound. Fatherhood is a difficult thing.

The venom numbs me to any pain. Gets me high in a way that nothing else could, all I can do is moan and grasp at the ground. Crack my fingernails against the gravel, because my spilled brain is soaking into my hair, climbing up into the follicles, tickling on the way back in. I vomit a half foam puddle onto the ground and laugh, then I vomit again. It wafts up from the cement like Cola, like red wine, like diesel smoke on the highway.

Someone sits me up and calls security. The next steps all happen concurrently, like still lifes pasted onto one scrapbook page.

The bargain-priced knitting of hospital sheets scratches my back as one of the EMTs picks me up, the puddle of my liquified brain crusty between my fingers.

I feel the cold night air before I even leave, see the hospital lights glaring above me when I face the ground.

Scoop some of my brain up, pour it back into my head with a funnel. You can't let me leave without it, I tell them.

Put my two hands together in prayer but the angels in navy collars shake their heads no, it's just blood, what's your name, they ask. The talking one holds my neck up on his palms while the other stands above me, shining sun into my eyes. The one with the palms, he looks like a tuskless elephant.

Snake baby decides to exercise then, its lithe body desperate to separate my flesh from skin and devour this elephant whole, to go one way then the other, trace the blue vessels transporting my blood with its whole body, to get lost in the stream and try to tear its way out, rip open the skin at the seams, squeeze out between the pores.

The light sanitizes me, slaps me awake as the pain takes over the high and when they ask me what my name is, I tell them there's a fucking snake inside me but they repeat themselves so I say my name is Ames and the whole time, Snake baby keeps on moving around, rearranging my nerves and muscles. I want to move my left leg but Snake baby has disconnected that part, paralyzed it internally. Everything else is a tangled mess of actions, movement is quizzical and impractical, my limbs sparking wired cords unplugged from their sockets.

Snake baby calms down a bit, scared of the light. Snake baby never meant trouble, so it coils up around my small intestine, says sorry through a dance along the anatomy, says it'll keep its mouth shut, fangs sheathed.

I'm telling my angels all of this in the ambulance, serenaded by the sirens and flashing red and blues. They half hang onto my moans, half stare at the hard road ahead of us.

Snake baby's not such a bad guy, I just messed up, I tell them. Tripped a little bit, fell back onto old concrete.

Snake baby, why'd you do that, I ask. *Snake baby, why can't you just use your words?*

Snake baby, the only thing I want is for you to love me. All I want is to crush up your venom and inhale it, feel it fog up my head and turn me into a dancing star, see the strobe lights wash over me.

Snake baby responds by curling up onto itself into a sailor's knot. It wraps its tail around its stomach and falls over.

C'mon Snake baby, I didn't mean to hurt your feelings.

By the time we reach the hospital, the emergency room, the high has faded into muted grays. My head pounds and threatens to split, pressure building at the wound ready to blow like steam gasping out of a pipe. Snake baby's asleep, has been since we reached the hospital. I tell the physician in front of me one last time that there's a snake baby inside me.

I lift my shirt up and point to the left of my belly button, where one of the kidneys should be I think, and ask him to feel it, take his fingers into my own and poke them against the fat. His fingers are cold and dry, wrapped up in a latex glove. He tells me he doesn't feel anything, but I insist, I persevere, I ask him to cut me open. Let me have your scalpel, I ask, if you're not gonna do much about it. He asks me what I've had to drink, any drugs in my system, and I say no Doc, 'course not Doc, but he says he can smell it through his mask, don't you lie to me. You calling me a liar? I ask him and he says absolutely, I'm absolutely saying you're lying, I need you to tell me how much you've had. Alcohol and anesthetics don't mix, he adds. Haven't had anything to drink, got some venom in me though, I respond. He lets out a sigh like frost from a freezer, smoke falling loose from his lips.

What kind of venom, he asks, though I haven't thought about it until now.

What kind of snake are you, Snake baby? You a King Cobra? You're too small, your length sits snug between my elbow and my forearm, you're no bigger than my hand stretched from end to end.

I don't know, I tell the Doc, and he gets mad. He storms off, kicks up color as he walks away, leaves me all alone in the waiting room. *Now that*, I tell Snake baby, *is childish.*

Across from me, a woman with a bulging belly stares at the space where the physician used to be. I point at her, point at my own belly, tell her I get it, it's a pain this one, and she just nods at me. Snake baby coils around my heart in embarrassment, like a hose tangled around its reel.

What are you gonna name it, I ask her.

She looks away, averts her eyes like she's ashamed of me. Maybe she is.

I ask her again, and this time she shifts toward me. She takes me in, dissects me cell by cell. This autopsy hurts almost as much as when Snake baby bites.

Her, she says, emphasizing the pronoun, name is Eve.

Pretty name, I think.

My mama named me Ames, I say. S'posed to be French for friend.

That's a delightful name, she says. And she believes it. A smile slips out, creasing the skin at the corner of the mouth.

Sorry for talking so much, I say.

She nods, and turns away. The two of us are silent now.

Hey, Snake baby?

Its tail stands tall and raps on my shoulder like a solicitor on his last house, tired and weary of shut doors.

I love you. I'll love you 'til my heart runs out. You know that, don't you?

Snake baby's tongue flickers in response and I stop to think about how nice it would be if Snake baby could talk to me, and I could talk back. We'd talk about the way we met, cradle the words between us and share them, taking turns dipping into language. Maybe Snake baby would even laugh the silly kind of laugh, the kind that makes you giggle just from hearing it.

It takes a few moments for me to be released from the hospital. I say bye to the nice lady, and she nods at me, waves me goodbye. Everything's worn off now: the pain, the suffocation and electric closeness with death, Snake baby's injected high. All that's left is a tired me, and I find my way home past closed eyes.

I take another shower, rinsing the vomit and blood off of myself. Hadn't cracked anything, they'd told me, just a little bit of blood, nothing that the antee-beeotics wouldn't take care of. The nurse had an accent with pull, and it tugged me in. Almost asked for her number, but Snake baby, good boy, ran down my stomach and into that place, and strung me up tight. I excused myself, and he saved me from embarrassment.

Lying in bed, I imagine Snake baby sitting on my kidneys now, rolled up like scotch tape waiting to be pulled apart.

Snake baby, I need you more than I need myself.

It disagrees and shifts, pressing down on my bladder, and I stand up to walk to the bathroom but pause when I see the bottle and its ragged cellophane label on my nightstand. And I know this is wrong but I hold its neck and choke it out, and I slip its open lips onto mine, scouring its throat for a trace of life or being, waiting for sand to rise in an hourglass, waiting for a corpse to rise from its coffin to remind me of medicine, of love, to teach me how to rear Snake baby up so it will not find itself buried in grain liquor in the next life.

But the drop remains suspended in gaseous flight, forever evaporated into the bottle's biome, and I search for the stains it might have left because I am desperate for its spirit but Snake baby, as if reaching for home, climbs up the esophagus and grips it tight, spiraling up each organ in ladder-fashion. I curl over in pain as it reaches the stomach and the bile follows, pulled up by the tight knot of Snake baby's body. Clutching my mouth, I throw the bottle to the floor and run to the bathroom.

Everything comes loose and the lights exhale above me, door ajar to allow in air and I gasp and gasp and gasp, but Snake baby never lets up so I go again as the faucet stares down at me in stoic judgment, and my eyes look up at me against the water, begging for more.

The breathing comes late, and night has already swung into motion. Outside, a boy calls for someone, has tripped and bruised himself. His crying mixes into the air until I am unable to discern it from my own breathing, the controlled rhythm of exhalation and expulsion that dictates my life or death on this tiled floor, next to a toilet full of vomit.

You there, Snake baby?

It sits in my skull, searching for a dark corner to curl into so it can fall into a deep and anxious slumber.

127

Three Chairs
Naoko Fujimoto

Poetry

NATIONALITY Japanese
FIRST LANGUAGE Japanese
SECOND LANGUAGE English

Previously unpublished

The first time war sat next to me was not after I had listened to a Nagasaki atomic bomb survivor at dinner. It was when a Georgian said, "My cousin saw your guys shoot one of ours." A Russian covered her eyes and stood there in the kitchen.   Neither of them opened their doors the next morning when I ate my honey toast. We were roommates.

How We Said Goodbye
Yanita Georgieva

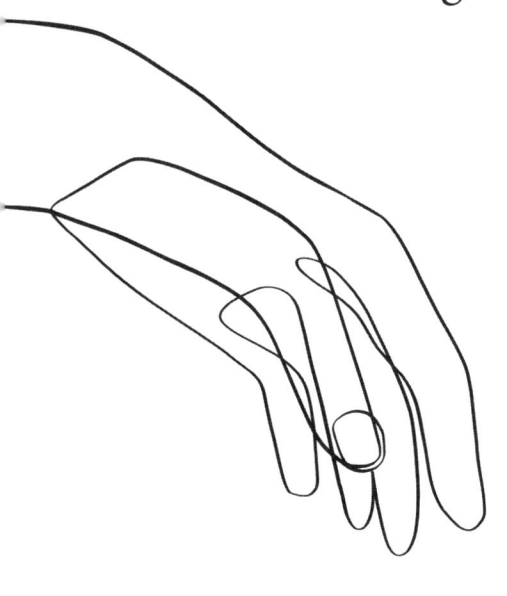

Poetry

NATIONALITY Bulgarian
FIRST LANGUAGE Bulgarian
SECOND LANGUAGES English, Arabic & Italian

Appeared in Issue Fall '20

Five men with footballer haircuts and off-brand tracksuits
buried my grandfather in a two-metre grave.

Before that, they dug up my father
and tucked him by his feet. I kept my glasses off,

listened to a man of god who'd memorised
his lines. Did he know about the end?

Even when your mouth and mind
defied you, you stretched your fingers out

and counted what was missing from the garden:
apples, figs, and *that long yellow thing*.

I think you would have liked a room with bright
green pictures of the otherworldly.

I think you would have liked to decompose and feed
the roots of something grand and worthy

like a peach tree or tomato plant, ripe
with history, plump with giving, every bite a sacrifice.

Into Something Rich and Strange

Lisa Giacalone

Poetry

NATIONALITY Italian & German
FIRST LANGUAGE German
SECOND LANGUAGES English & Italian

Appeared in Issue Fall '23

There's a house on the hills of Segesta.
    A hand
    so wet,
        it drips when it knocks.
    Passioned plastic, porcelain mothers
        nail their wooden sons to the cross.

There's a house on the hills of Segesta.
    The gas stove's leaking taste,
    saline.
    Brack water,
        black
            brine fed to us in the mornings.
        Long
            have the Gods been drowned.

There's a house on the hills of Segesta.
    She called
        from beneath;
    Our father heard her
    calling, too:
        He cried out from the shore,
            he knew, yes, he knew.

There's a house on the hills of Segesta.
    So you
        went — you were wicked —
    you had to die.
    You
        would breathe water.
    You went under and I —

There's a house on the hills of Segesta.

Evenings in Monroe Apartments
Gladwell Pamba

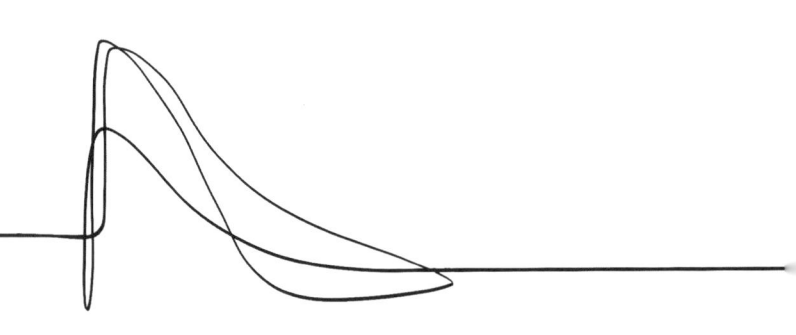

Flash Fiction

NATIONALITY Kenyan
FIRST LANGUAGE Swahili
SECOND LANGUAGE English

Appeared in Issue Fall '21

Every evening after dinner, mum perched in front of the dressing mirror and drew her brows with a black eye pencil, applied the red lipstick, and when her trembling hands held the eyeliner, she leaned close to the mirror as if about to kiss her reflection. When she faced me, I met an angry or flat or excited face, depending on how thick or long she'd drawn the brows.

"Will Empress Lily turn heads and enter cars?" she asked. I nodded and she smiled tightly. "Are you sure the cat eye is sharp enough?"

She looked at her arse in the reflection, pushed it back, arched her back and stood on one foot.

Before she stepped out of the house, she said, "You will not open the door for anybody. Not even Jesus when he knocks."

Stroking my cheeks, she reminded me to turn off the lights at 9 p.m. Her hug left a tickling sensation in my nose and her perfume lingered on my chest for hours. Mum's thudding stilettos faded from the second floor down the winding staircase to the cabro. *Tap! Tap! Tap!* Before getting into the taxi, she pulled down her sequined mini-dress, looked up, waved at me and blew cherry-red kisses. I snatched them from the air, the tiny invisible butterflies, clinging to them until she returned. Every time the taxi vroomed down the street, the desire to go with her exploded in my gut, consuming me. I fought back the stinging tears and the screaming absence. It felt as though mum folded air in her clutch bag and went away with it, leaving me gasping to stay alive.

For hours after her departure, I remained on the same spot, kneeling on the couch and staring outside our apartment building. Mr. Murgor came home from work; Liam's dog ran after fireflies on the lawn; smoke rose from Mrs. Kimani's patio and the Rudolfs drove out for dinner — to the Debonairs or the Pizza Inn along Ngong Road, probably.

When the clock chimed *twinkle twinkle little star* at 9 o'clock, I turned off all the lights. I watched the night thin out. The downstairs neighbour staggered to his room, leaning on the door and fumbling with the lock, the Rudolfs' Range Rover blasted music as they disembarked and Mrs. Kimani exhausted her pack of cigarettes. When everyone in Monroe Apartments eventually switched off their lights, the night felt abandoned as life curled behind quiet walls.

The air held a certain kind of dense chill after hours of staring outside. I wrote my name on the blurry window panes and blew hot air on them, rubbed off the name, rewrote, rubbed, rewrote until the approaching taxi pulled over on the kerb and dropped off mum. I tiptoed to my bed, holding my teddy tight and my eyes closed. I only knew it was morning when mum planted butterflies on my forehead, stripped the window naked, letting the sun fill my bedroom, saying, "Anthony, darling, time for school."

One evening, the air turned dense and chill again, and I wrote my name on the panes. Blew air on it, rubbed it off, rewrote, rubbed off. I wrote all my classmates' names and rubbed them off, rewrote. I watched Mr. Murgor drive in from work and back out, watched Liam lock his German Shepherd in its kennel, watched Mrs. Kimani open the screen door. I watched until my school bus hooted and hooted, and eventually left. As the neighbourhood bustled with life, my head pounded, my stomach grumbled and my ears craved for the sound of mum's approaching taxi, but that never happened.

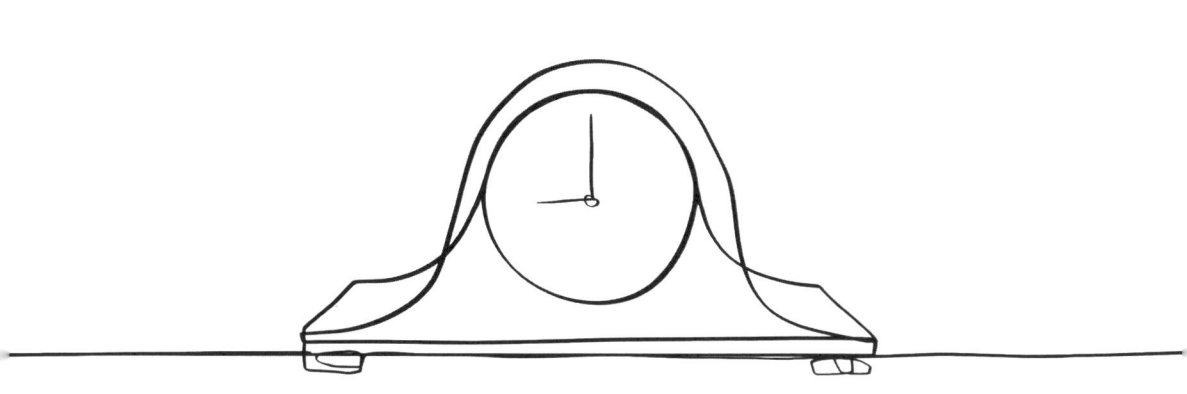

The River-Song
Susmita Paul

Fiction

NATIONALITY Indian
FIRST LANGUAGE Bengali
SECOND LANGUAGES English, Hindi & German

Previously unpublished

In the voice of thunder he begins the telling of the epic, picking up from where he had left off yesterday.

The floods, by Nature enemies to land,
And proudly swelling with their new command,
Remove the living stones that stopp'd their way…

In the middle of the night, she had to go pee-pee. Rubbing her eyes, she sat up in the *charpoy*. Datta was rumbling. She had asked the NGO *dada*, when would the new toilet be set up in her home. He had said, next year, if not this year. *Baba* was sleeping deeply. With sleepy steps, wobbling and yet knowing the way, she went to the tree standing on the high land near her thatched mud house. Facing the other houses in her village, she squatted under the tree and relieved herself. Datta was rumbling too much, she thought to herself.

    She stood up and looked at the river. Under the quiet and cloudy night sky, there seemed to be smoke arising from it in the distance.

…and gushing from their source, augment the sea.

Then, with his mace, their monarch struck the ground.
With inward trembling, Earth receiv'd the wound,

and rising streams a ready passage found.
Th' expanded waters gather on the plain,...

She started walking back towards her home, where *Baba* was sleeping, where Munia, her rag doll, was at watch, protecting her from all the monsters of the night. Her feet increased their pace.

...
Then rushing onwards, with a sweepy sway,
bear flocks, and folds, and lab'ring hinds away...

Now, tears trickle down her rough brown cheeks.

Baba had promised that she would start going to school next year. His business of carrying logs from the mangroves was going well. *Kaku*, the owner of the van in which he used to transport the logs, had also promised a greater percentage from the revenue earned. *Baba* had even bought a new toy comb for Munia.

The teacher looks at the children of all ages as they sit around him, listening to Ovid's *Metamorphoses*. She is crying. Some of the other children's eyes look vacant, lost in the memory of last night. In the candle light, their shadows on the walls are tall. In Pakhiralay village, evenings are the time of telling stories — of remembering the dead.

She was found holding on to the topmost branch of the tree under which she had relieved herself the night before. The greater part of the tree was submerged in the river. Sixteen families lost their homes that night. She lost *Baba* and Munia.

...now seas and Earth were in confusion lost,
A world of waters, and without a coast...

...
At length the world was all restor'd to view;
But desolate, and of a sickly hue:
Nature beheld her self, and stood aghast,
A dismal desert, and a silent waste,...

The village has adopted her. She lives with the sixteen uprooted families in the only *pucca* house in the village: the school building. The teacher, with his dense beard, reminds her of her *Baba*. The stories from this epic that he is telling make her feel sad.

She is alone in the overcrowded hall.

As his voice trails off, the teacher remembers the romanticism with which he had read Ovid for the first time. He came to Pakhiralay village seven weeks after Datta river had changed its course for the third time this year. The school he was supposed to teach at has been transformed into a shelter. He has no place to teach but this one.

As she tries to sleep, a line from the epic that the teacher told keeps coming back to her: *I want to speak about bodies changed into new forms.*

For the first time in a long, long time, she wants to do something. Something other than feeling sad about *Baba* and Munia. She starts humming a folk tune softly.

I want to sing the song of the river
I want to sing the song of Datta   now
I want to sing the song of dreams
I want to sing the song of things
That matter—
I want to sing the song of life
And death hanging from a tree
I want to sing the song of life
And death in stories long ago
I want to sing the song of change   today
Today
Today

Two Possibilities for Shylock

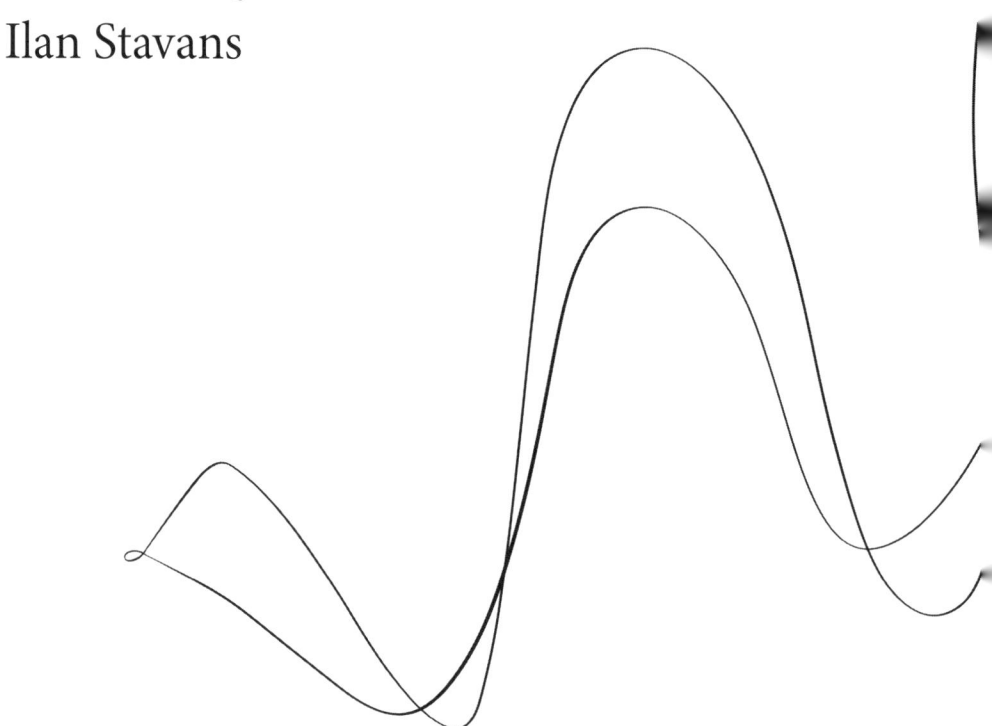

Ilan Stavans

Poetry

NATIONALITY   Mexican, U.S. & Polish
FIRST LANGUAGES   Yiddish & Spanish
SECOND LANGUAGES   English, Hebrew, Ladino, French & Spanglish

Previously unpublished

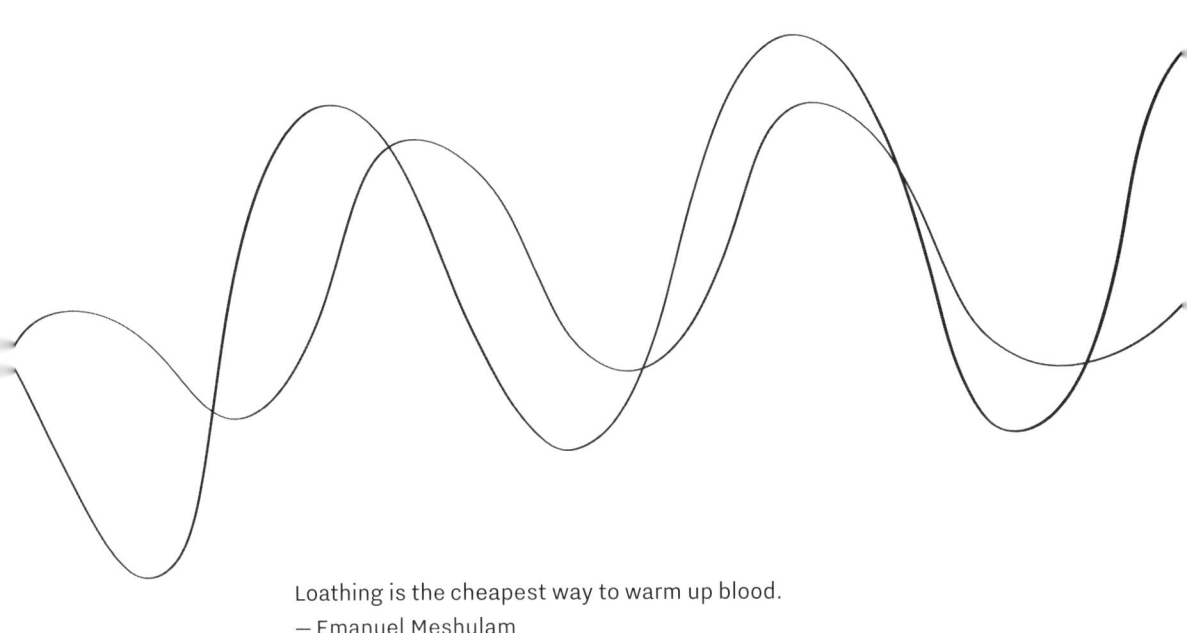

> Loathing is the cheapest way to warm up blood.
> — Emanuel Meshulam

"Art thou contented, Jew?" Portia asks Shylock in Act IV, Scene 1. His answer: "I pray you give me leave to go from hence. I am not well."

There are still two acts to go in *The Merchant of Venice.* Had Shakespeare finished it here, he would have left Venice unequivocally triumphant. But he adds insult to injury when Jessica absconds with Lorenzo and Shylock's co-religionaries in Cannaregio show no signs of life.

Still, by the end of the play Shylock's fate is left open. What next?

Two possibilities. In the first, Shylock and his spouse Hagar—named after Abraham's second wife and the mother of Ishmael in Genesis—do as they are told at the trial: In the picturesque Venice of gondolas, *traghetti*, and double ducats, they convert to Christianity after bequeathing their estate. Bitter, broken, and alone, Shylock dies of the plague.

In the second possibility, Jessica, after a brief failed marriage to Lorenzo, apologizes for her elopement, reacquaints herself with her father, who, after the death of Hagar, is now a *marrano* fluent in *sefardí*, the language of his ancestors. Her two sons Rehoboam and Jehoahaz go on rejecting Shylock, who insists on reminding them that Antonio "disgraced me… scorned my nation… heated mine enemies."

After Jehoahaz Benveniste converts back to Judaism, he engages in friendship with other Jews in the Venice ghetto. In 1610, he owns a fleet of commercial ships crisscrossing the Mediterranean Sea and amasses a fortune. He donates a portion of it in support of Talmud yeshivas in Greece and the Balkans.

In 1807, Tilde Vital Benveniste, the great granddaughter of Jehoahaz Benveniste's fifth child, is an Alsace Jew devoted to the education reform in France. Along with her two sons, she reeducates the way Napoleon envisions it in his letter to his Minister of the Interior, Jean-Baptiste de Nompère de Champagny, First Duc de Cadore, stating that "to reduce, if not destroy, the tendency of Jewish people to be harmful to civilization, it is necessary to change them."

The reeducation fails. A century on, Shylock's lineage is still traceable to playwright Letizia Pincherle Maurogonato, author of the manifesto *L'educazione israelita*, and, thereafter, to an astronomy student in Pisa, Adele Abecassis, who, as an adult, is a Hebraist who finances the first Dutch translation of *The Passover Haggadah*.

Shylock's final heir is Solomon Fresco, the editor of *El Tiempo*, a Ladino-language newspaper in Istanbul, known for, among other tasks, exposing anti-Semites. In his last week of life, Fresco attends an adaptation of *Der Yiddisher Kenig Lear* in Warsaw, then travels back home, where his throat is slashed outside his home in the neighborhood of Balat, on a warm September night in 1897.

A sentence written with chuck by his anonymous assassin on a naked wall reads — in English: "Are you happy, Jew?"

jailmaze
Maja Ulasik

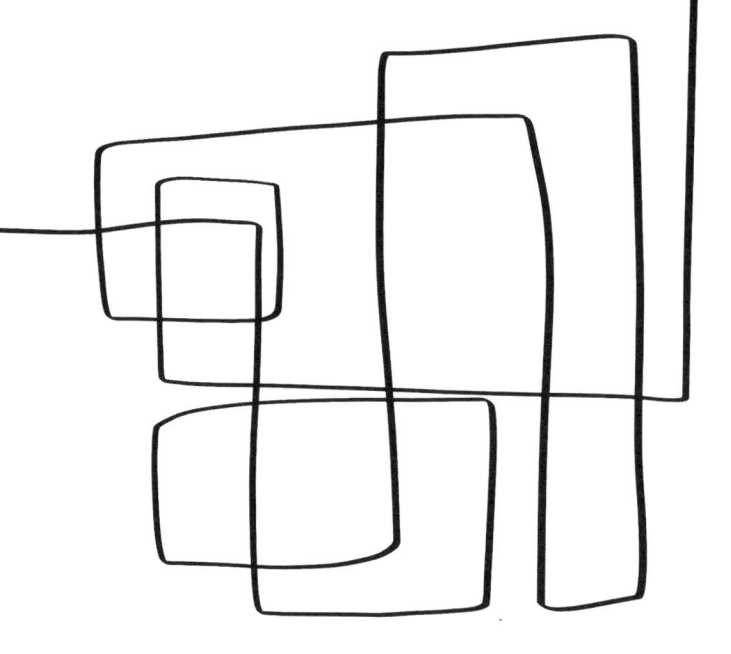

Flash Fiction

NATIONALITY Polish
FIRST LANGUAGE Polish
SECOND LANGUAGES English, French, German, Swedish & Norwegian

Appeared in Issue Fall '21

mornings are sunny, afternoons are cloudy, you never know about evenings, but nights are full of dreams.

you can open a window even though you are in a prison that is also a labyrinth, which is a beautiful word but a fascinating and horrifying concept.

when you open the window, chirps fill your ears, and it comes as a surprise because you think and have always thought that it's not possible to hear any beautiful sound while being in a prison or a labyrinth, or a place that is both a prison and a labyrinth and is called a jailmaze.

believe it or not, the birds can sing everywhere; what's more: crows' favorite place is a cemetery.

talking about birds: those that sing just outside of the jailmaze sound colorful. now, don't make a face. it's cloudy at night but they don't take offence. they sing days and nights. they sing matinees and lullabies.

all it takes is to open the window, an ear or two, and listen, and... it's parrots! it's better to close your eyes because you don't see the walls, floors and ceilings of your jailmaze, and you can imagine it doesn't exist and you're actually somewhere in the tropics. if you expose your firmly closed eyelids to the sun, you will discover that light doesn't respect the thin fragile curtains that are covering your eyes but daringly shines through so that you can believe that you are in the tropics and tropics are hot and free and everyone always dreams of tropics for some reason that is very difficult to understand.

nobody ever dreams of the jailmaze but many people nightmare about it, yet only few really understand it.

this text is a jailmaze and i'm in a jailmaze which is easy to deduct because it's impossible to write any other text in a jailmaze than a jailmaze itself. jailmaze jailmaze jailmaze.

(of course i could use capital letters, but i don't want to scare the parrots.)

here is a fact. i know how this all sounds: childish, kitschy and lunatic (which is a beautiful and horrifying word just like a labyrinth). but i have an argument: this is a jailmaze and a jailmaze is childish, kitschy, and lunatic.

the reason is that you cannot build a jailmaze out of reason. to put another human in a jail as well as to put another human in a maze is a very childish solution to any problem. it's also a bit kitschy, lacks style, and it seems obvious to everyone that paying attention to the design of a prison or a labyrinth would turn an inhuman idea into a bestial idea. and it's only a lunatic's mind that can develop a concept of so many walls in a space so beautiful and free like earth.

i am a lunatic because i build walls of letters into a paper of plain and white which is almost as beautiful as a summer sky. my letters are black, and they have horrifying shapes like *t h i s*. why would i write on this earth while i can walk on this earth, touch the grass with my bare feet, let the sun shine through my eyelids right into my soul, and listen to parrots chirping in the sweet moment on earth that i have been given for free and only for a while.

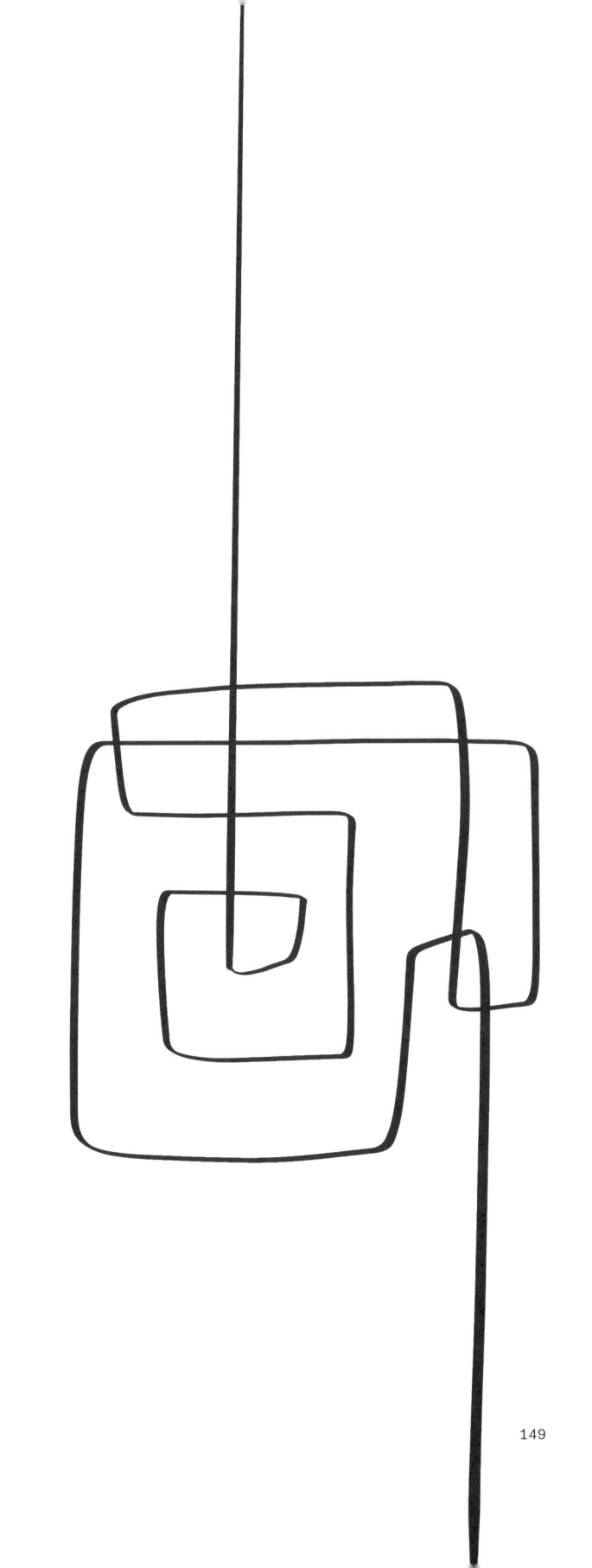

For Your Own Good

Huina Zheng

Nonfiction

NATIONALITY Chinese
FIRST LANGUAGES Hakka Dialects, Mandarin & Cantonese
SECOND LANGUAGE English

Appeared in Issue Spring '23

Normally, in my country of China, the news reports you saw were positive, and people did not post negative comments on social media about society and government. I had believed my country was different and it was getting better because of all the positive news reports. But since the outbreak of the Coronavirus epidemic in early 2020, lots of "ridiculous" and "surreal" posts had leaked out — they would be gone within a day — and then the world remained safe and stable again.

The health workers clubbed a woman's three dogs to death after she tested positive and was put into quarantine.

The neighborhood committee forced a 98-year-old man to vaccinate, leading him to die of a vaccine reaction.

A high school expelled a student because he failed to notify the school that his parents returned home from another city, violating epidemic prevention regulations.

Posts and videos abound, some more "absurd" than others. No one could explain these phenomena, so more and more people on social media stated that there must be foreign forces behind all of these incidents — "…they tried to overthrow our government and take advantage. We must always be on guard against falling into the trap of the evil capitalist countries."

I knew that the real world I lived in differed from the official world. Still, under the long-term official guidance of ideology, public opinion, and news immersion, the boundary between these two worlds had blurred. All these posts were slaps in the face. The bubble exploded.

I asked a friend I trusted, "Why are we like this?"

She replied, "Because we don't know anything else."

We were both silent — we had to stop the conversation before it led us too far away.

The silence brought back memories of my younger years when I struggled to make sense of the world.

I grew up in a traditional family in southern China — my father was the master of the house, and my mother was a housewife. My father was hot-tempered. If my siblings and I disturbed him, he would shout, "Stop it! Or I will beat you to death, dig a hole in the hill and bury you." I never thought it was a threat; I believed it was a fact.

My parents thought children were too young to understand things, so they never minded we were around when they talked. From my mother's chitchat with relatives, I learned that an uncle accidentally beat his son to death. I had always known that sons and daughters were different. What chance did a daughter have if a parent could beat his exalted son to death? My father had a factory on the outskirts — we were a minute's walk from the mountains — I feared he would beat me to death in a rage, and when my family moved, I would be left alone and forgotten. Consequently, I developed the instinct to read my father's expression to detect any hints of rage.

My family moved to a small town when I was ten. My father ran a factory in our hometown, so he was thankfully seldom home. My siblings and I never missed him or asked about him. My mother liked to joke that we were like little mice around a cat when my father was home. She was right. How could a mouse not hold its breath around a cat that might devour it?

This fear did me some good when I went to school. Beating children was not considered violence but a way for parents and teachers to discipline. My teachers would hit our palms with a ruler or pinch us if we didn't behave.

On the first day of school in fifth grade, my classmates were chatting and laughing. A man in his early thirties entered the classroom. He had fair skin, a crew cut, and a mustache on his lips. Some classmates were still making noise. He pursed his lips, and his face twitched. He said in an almost calm voice, "I am your Chinese and homeroom teacher, and my last name is Yang. Today is the first class, and not everyone is disciplined.

Doesn't matter. There is time for me to make all of you disciplined." Teacher Yang did not yell to warn us, but beneath his calm appearance, I felt unease. I was right — this was the calm before the storm.

He began to beat us on the second day and every day for the rest of our school year.

If he spotted you not concentrating or chatting, he either walked toward you and struck your face with his hand or demanded that you step to the platform so he could slap you. If he asked a question and you failed to know the answer, he tweaked your ear. He hit you if he saw you playing when you were supposed to study. That was what he did to a boy in the class. On a Saturday afternoon, when he saw the boy skateboarding in the square near the school, he punched him. "You will have a unit test next week. Have you finished your homework? Have you studied for the exam? How dare you not study! Keep this in mind. Whenever I catch you playing, I will beat you," he warned the whole class.

You couldn't do well yourself to avoid being beaten. We had row-and-column seating in the classroom — the class was divided into different columns. If students in your column did not behave, Teacher Yang would punish all students in the same column. He would order us to study the textbook while he took the time to beat each of us. He would start with the students sitting in the front row. If your face was not toward him, he would yank your hair or your ear if your hair was too short, turn your face toward him, and hit you on the cheek. Sometimes a slap was not enough to ease his anger — he would pull you and your deskmate's hair and bump your heads toward each other. "Thump," "thump," and "thump." You saw stars for several seconds.

The worst part was not when he hit you but moments before he did. I would open my Chinese textbook and pretend to study the text. Out of the corner of my eye, I saw him approaching. I held my breath and got prepared. Before I knew it, it was over. You felt pain and a burning sensation, but it would fade. It was not that bad. But the class was not over yet. Even if the class ended, as the homeroom teacher, Teacher Yang would still return before school was over and punish you when he believed you did something wrong. Even though the day was over, on the next school day, it started all over again.

Each time he graded test papers, he would sit in front of the platform, holding a ferule, and the whole class waited for their turn to walk toward him with the graded examination paper. He would look at our examination papers and hit our palms according to our grades. The lower scores you got, the more beating you had. Once Teacher Yang used a broomstick to beat us. The broomstick must have cracked from the numerous hitting, so when he struck a girl's palm, the crack in the broomstick cut her palm, and she bled. That day, he walked home with the girl to explain to her parents what had happened.

The following morning, he told us that the girl's parents said to him that a strict teacher produced outstanding students. They were grateful that their daughter had such a strict teacher. Teacher Yang should not worry. They would understand even if he broke their daughter's hand to discipline her. When Teacher Yang recounted it, his face lit up with pride.

He implemented corporal punishment while our math teacher (I don't remember her name), a middle-aged woman, applied mental penalty. She disliked girls in general and especially hated girls poor at math. She liked to compare them to pigs.

In class, she would point at a girl and say in a loud voice that the whole class could hear, "You are so stupid. A pig is smarter than you. Why don't you quit school and find yourself a husband?" And then she would continue to bully another girl. "Do you have a brain? Did a pig eat your brain?"

Boys laughed and clapped, and those girls lowered their heads. I feared Teacher Yang, but I resented the math teacher.

Once Teacher Yang took us on a one-day autumn trip to the Martyrs' Cemetery and said we should write a composition. It was not far away from the school. We lined up to walk back to school in the evening. One car had to stop when we crossed the street, and the horn blared several times. Teacher Yang went over, and the car window lowered. Teacher Yang said something to the car owner with a smile, but the car owner wagged his hand, and the window rose. Teacher Yang's face twitched — the sign of his suppressed rage. When we returned to school, past the school hours, he still asked us to stay. He pointed out things we had done wrong during the day, and each student took turns getting beaten up.

I usually did well in my studies, but once I failed a Chinese unit test. Teacher Yang hit me harder than usual because, as a good student, I had let him down, and he wanted me to learn my lesson. My palms were swollen all afternoon.

Students who had failed the test should ask their parents to meet the teacher the next day. I was not worried that my mother would punish me for failing a test because she believed an elementary school education was sufficient for girls. Instead I feared she would not go to school. In that case, Teacher Yang would surely punish me. It was Friday, so I had a weekend to work out a solution.

There was a multiple-choice question that I got right, but Teacher Yang put an X on it, deducting two points. If I could tell Teacher Yang about it, with the returning two points, my grade would be 61, not 59. Then I passed the test, and my mother did not need to go to school. But how could I tell Teacher Yang? In those days, we did not have mobile phones, and I did not know his landline number. I told two friends about it. One of them told me that she knew where he lived and she could take me to meet him. To boost my courage, the other friend would also go with me.

We set off the next day, but I hesitated before his house. I dared not ring the bell. What would he think about it? Would he be offended and beat all of us?

"Come on. I know his history," my friend said. She told us that Teacher Yang borrowed money from her father to buy this house, and he was still in debt. He beat his wife so severely that she ran away, leaving behind their son. Now Teacher Yang beat his son every day until the boy was black and blue.

I recalled my father's rage and felt a sharp pang of pain. If a father would badly beat his son, what chance would I, his student, have? How could I expect compassion?

I decided to go home. Being beaten by Teacher Yang was not that bad. I could grit my teeth and endure it. At least he would never accidentally beat me to death. Teacher Yang did not scar me; my continued dread for my father overshadowed my fear for Teacher Yang.

No one ever told us that it was wrong for teachers to beat students. If you told your parents about it, they would ask you to reflect on what you had done wrong to deserve it. Naturally, I never told my parents.

It had been our fine tradition to esteem teachers and education for thousands of years. As students, you should always respect and obey teachers; you should never question or challenge them. If your teacher told you the sun rose in the west, you nodded as if you agreed. Punishment was necessary to make students good, just as teachers assigned homework so students could learn.

Teacher Yang dedicated himself to teaching and imparting knowledge. Although he seldom smiled, when we did well, he would nod with a proud smile and urge us to continue to work hard. He was like a strict father — when you played the piano, he would stand beside you and hit your arm with a ruler whenever you played a wrong note — all to make you improve your skills. It was for your own good. You should be grateful. We should respect Teacher Yang and thank him for his selfless dedication. In some way I think my classmates and I learned to blame ourselves. We believed corporal punishment and abuse were common in school learning, so we never discussed it.

There were three worlds I lived in — the real world, the official world we were taught to believe we lived in, and the third world that I created for myself. The third world contained all the alternatives. Every night before I fell asleep, I imagined different versions of the day's events — the girl's parents asking Teacher Yang to apologize for beating their daughter, and the boy who got slapped for skateboarding fighting back.

In the official world, everything was sanitized to seem pleasant. The textbooks and news revolved around this world. You only saw positive things — all parents loved their children, and all teachers were responsible and caring. We were trained to believe in this world and obey.

Some of my middle and high school teachers continued to abuse students, but my impeccable grades formed a shield around me, dispelling their humiliation. Your grades determined whether you deserved respect or not.

When I entered puberty, I became silent. I put myself into a jar so that it blocked out all my emotions. The real world would not affect me. However, the negative feelings I suppressed still found a way to sneak into the jar and haunted me. I wondered: Were there legitimate pains and rage others felt? What did they look like?

I read books. Teachers and parents believed that students should focus on studying in those years. Students were not allowed to read non-textbooks. Still, I devoured books, especially foreign literature. Strangely, the suffering in the corrupt, evil capitalist countries did not appall me. Instead, I felt understood, connected, and empowered — I saw another way of being — I felt *normal*. In the worlds created by foreign literature I felt I knew how to feel and think, but once I closed the book, I was not so sure.

I thought corporal punishment and emotional abuse only existed in rural areas or small towns, and that it only happened in the past or to students living in poverty. I was wrong.

A few years ago, when my sister's daughter went to kindergarten, my mother told me that because my niece was so active, her teacher tied her hands with a rope. "Don't you think it is wrong for the teacher to do so?" I asked my mother. But she laughed and said, "Your niece is so naughty, and the teacher is just bad-tempered."

A friend who sent her son to an expensive private elementary school told me that her son's classmate's parents had conflicts with the homeroom teacher. They suspected the teacher abused their daughter and asked the daughter to take a recording pen to school. According to the recording, the teacher indeed abused her.

However, when the parents demanded the school fire the teacher, no one supported them. In the end, they had to transfer their daughter to another school. "Aren't you worried the teacher might abuse your son too?" I asked the friend. She rolled her eyes.

I worked in an educational agency that helps Chinese students apply for overseas schools. The students all came from middle- and upper-class families. When I brainstormed with students about their personal statement, they shared their traumatic experiences, many of which happened in the classroom. A student told me he went to an elite elementary school, but because he always raised questions that disrupted the homeroom teacher's sense of discipline, he became the teacher's most disliked student. His mother only realized that he was bullied when one day in third grade his teacher told the class to line up to give him a slap. Another student told me that when he was in ninth grade, his teacher asked the class to vote for the student they would most like to kick out, and he got the highest votes. Their parents were educated and wealthy, but when the teachers bullied them, they did not help.

We now know it is wrong for teachers to abuse students, but why did these resourceful and educated parents remain silent? I realized I was so naïve. How could an individual fight against a system?

One day I read a news report that when a man met his former middle school teacher, a retired old man, in the street, he asked his teacher if he remembered how he used to humiliate and beat him. He slapped his teacher again and again. So many people carried the scars years into adulthood, but the teachers never thought much about it and continued abusing the next generation. The court sentenced the man to one year and a half in prison. My colleague commented, "How can you beat an old man, let alone a former teacher? Nuts!"

I said, "I had an elementary teacher who beat us every school day."

"That can't be true."

Of course, such things never happened in the official world. What point did I want to make? That I resented all teachers, or I'd developed an anti-social tendency? I shrugged and ended the conversation.

So often, I wanted to scream, and people would stare as if something was fundamentally wrong with me. I did not know how to feel and think in a *normal* way.

I'm a grown woman now, but I still try not to think of those years I spent in school. Before I graduated from college, my parents suggested I become a teacher — a safe and wise choice for girls, but I refused. I thought I would have to agree with the system and become an abuser if I wanted to be a teacher.

There is a kindergarten right next to my apartment. Perhaps the kids were too noisy or the teacher tried to avoid getting a sore throat from speaking out loud — so, she often used a loudspeaker to lecture students. When I worked in the room that was close to the kindergarten, I heard the teacher abuse the kids and yell at them.

I was restless and anxious the first day I sent my daughter to kindergarten. I immediately remembered how it felt — deep inside me, everything tightened up as if preparing my body for another blow. I had met the teachers, and they seemed nice, but I did not know who they were when alone with the kids. I still felt that tight, expectant tension all over my body. When I picked my daughter up from school, I noticed that she wore different pants. She told me that she had wetted the bed during the nap.

"What did your teacher say to you?" I asked.

"She said it didn't matter, and she would help me change the pants. She said so in a very nice and gentle way."

My tense nerves relaxed, and I could breathe again.

It struck me that I had prepared myself and my daughter for her to enter this system when she was still a baby. I read articles about how to use role-playing games or read signs of kids being abused. I taught her how to be polite at school and made sure that she was a role model student so teachers would all like her.

The Ministry of Education had long issued a code of professional ethics for teachers, one of the most important of which was that corporal punishment, including kicking and slapping, was forbidden. But varying degrees of punishment still existed. Posts about abuse spread throughout the Internet.

I tried to understand why we couldn't stop it. I speculated on many reasons — historical, cultural, systematic factors — but they were ungrounded. I could only find limited information, and the few articles I found just pecked at it. Whenever I brought up the subject, my friends and family remained silent or changed the topic; if I pushed, they became uncomfortable and told me it was only abnormal if I made a fuss about it.

My people were raised to believe in the merit of denial. The only way to overcome difficulties was to pretend they didn't exist so that we could have a future untainted by an unhappy past. For years I had to tell myself what happened at school was no big deal. The pain was just my imagination.

Self-denial did not liberate me but exacerbated my pain. I recalled how I felt when I read the 19-year-long struggle of Jean Valjean, the protagonist in *Les Miserables*. Valjean does nothing wrong, and he doesn't deserve to be oppressed, just as my classmates and I did not deserve to be abused. And it dawned on me, finally, that it had not been our fault. I felt relieved, a warm feeling flooding over me, as if someone held my hand and told me it was okay to think Teacher Yang should not beat us.

What if you were allowed to talk about it?

Would students who endured abuse learn that they were valued, we understood them, and it was not their fault?

Would the public understand that even though a teacher's slap did not leave a scar on the face, it did leave cracks in students' hearts?

Would we start to brainstorm solutions to prevent corporal punishment?

Schools reflected society. Perhaps many educated parents did not intervene because they knew that if this was the world we lived in, their children should learn to navigate the real world. The sooner, the better.

Or we all knew we could do nothing about it. Why torture yourself with things you could not stop? Better get numb and live your life.

A few days ago, I chatted over WeChat with a childhood friend in the same class with me in fifth and sixth grade. I asked if she still remembered Teacher Yang.

"Sure. My son will attend that school this September, and I just told him about Teacher Yang."

"What did you tell him?"

"Teacher Yang is a very strict teacher."

She was right. For a long time, when I thought of Teacher Yang, he was a responsible teacher. My friend had repositioned me in the right way to view Teacher Yang—a strict but well-intentioned teacher.

When the dogs' owner tested positive for Covid-19, officials thought the dogs might be positive too. The health workers clubbed the dogs to death so that the dogs would not spread the virus to people. They saved lives.

Likewise, the 98-year-old man could've died of Covid-19 if the resident committee had not forced him to vaccinate. They were doing their job, and took the trouble to care for the old man.

Similarly, the public should trust the government and follow the prevention and control measures. After all, we share the same goal—dynamic zero-Covid strategy. The student's parents should never violate the regulations.

When the sun rose to its highest, everything was clear and nice. See? There were indeed no shadows.

161

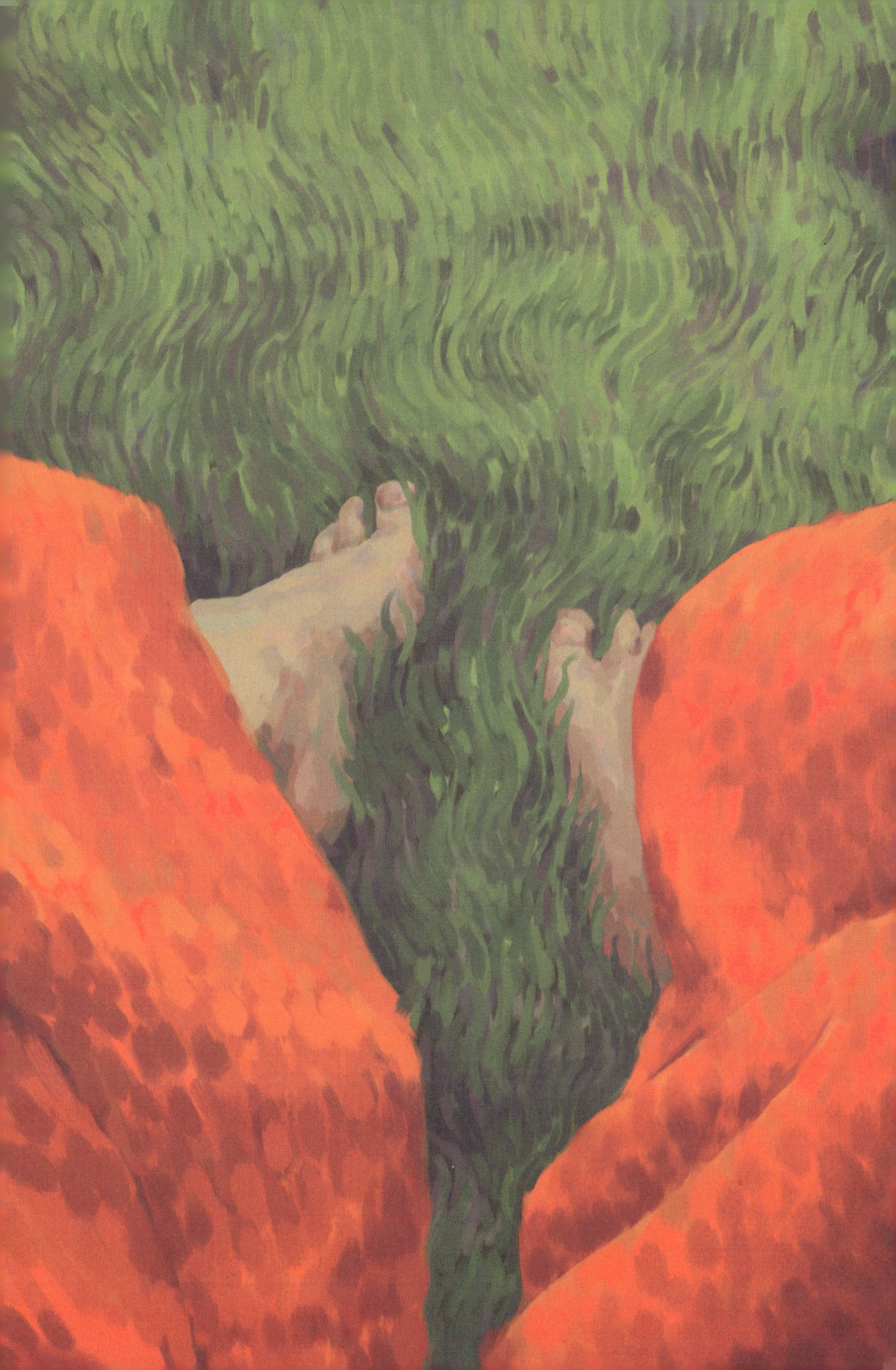

IDENTITIES

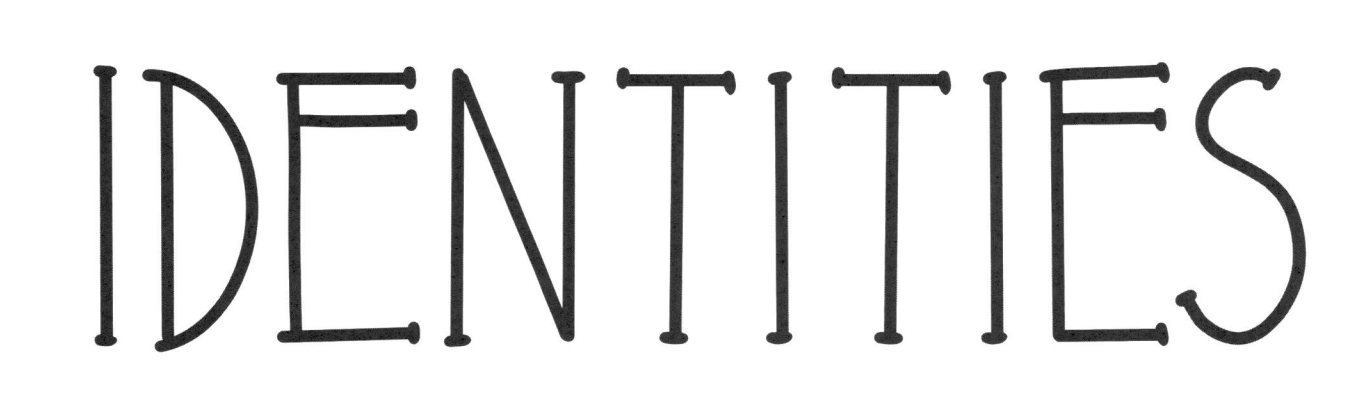

What is identity? It is interesting that we use this word in its singular form even though every human being is made up of a multitude of identities. There is no singular in this. This plurality is personal — something for every individual to figure out for themselves. It incorporates sexuality, ethnicity, class, and religion, among others.[16] Some of these facets we can choose while others are given to us through circumstance, birth, and other life events. Even if we cannot assemble all parts that constitute our multiple identities ourselves, we should always have the choice of how to express them. When it comes to ESL writers, we might first of all think of aspects such as ethnicity, cultural background, and origin that are discussed and put into focus.[17] However, like all humans, translingual authors have more to their identity than their nationality and culture. No person is only defined by their ethnicity or their sexuality. It is important that we as a society cease trying to devalue and reduce people to one distinct aspect of their identities. I, personally, am more than a white, heterosexual, cis-woman born in Austria. To understand the plurality of perspectives that see, feel, and try to understand the shared space we inhabit everyday, we need to stop labelling people based on what we think is most visible about them and become open to seeing the world through a variety of eyes.

This section of the anthology is shaped by a diversity of identities.

While the topic of sexuality and sexual orientation is the focus of "The River" among other texts, the nonfiction piece "The Hijab as a Red Herring" addresses religious identity. Likewise, the struggles that come with identity are highlighted, be it the childhood trauma a teenager experiences because her mother does not accept her sexual identity in "Coty 24" or the fact that one's accent reveals that you are not native and therefore treated as the Other in "A Brief Chronology of My English Accent." The people surrounding us, unfortunately at times also those that are supposed to support us, do not always accept our identities nor the way we decide to express them.

    Not only the difficulties of one's identities are addressed in the upcoming pieces, but you also get to see glimpses of a young woman's life with her friend, another woman's experience in a foreign country and how she arrives at decisions regarding her religious expression as well as poetic explorations of an I-persona's singularity and individuality. Finding our individual identities is a complex process and subject to constant change, and one of the most exciting things about it is that we can get closer to finding ourselves when we listen to other people's stories.

by Chiara Meitz

The Hijab as a Red Herring

Leila Aboulela

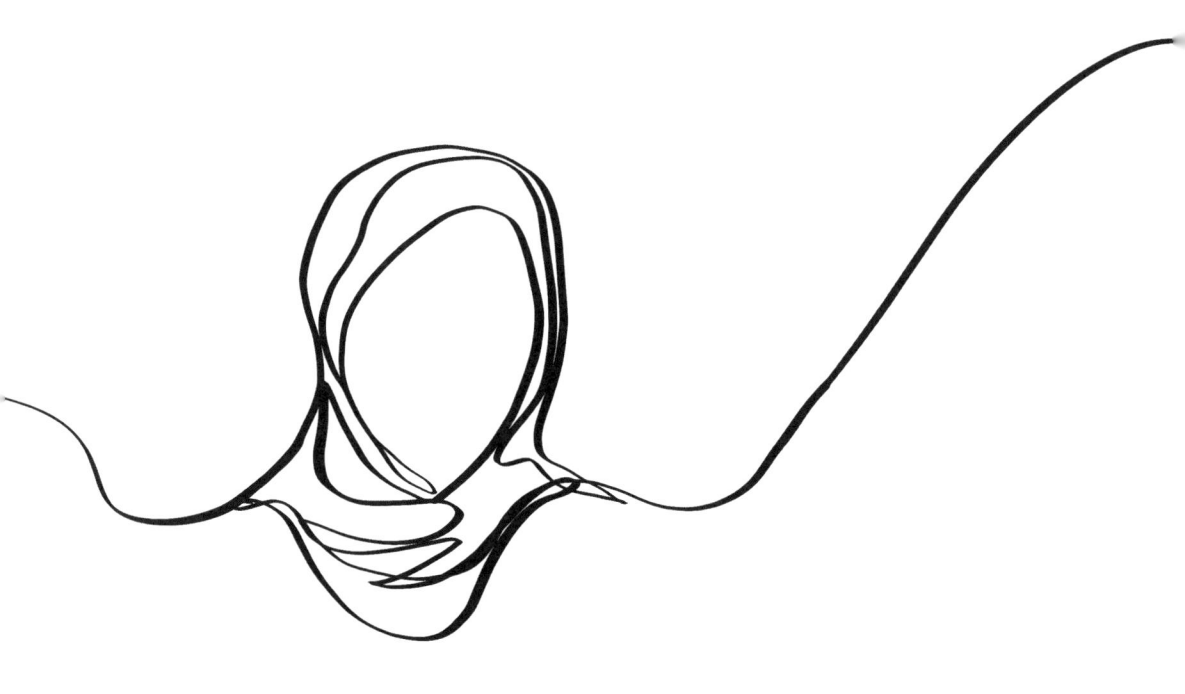

Nonfiction

NATIONALITY British
FIRST LANGUAGE Arabic
SECOND LANGUAGE English

Previously unpublished

In October 1987, a week into my first post-graduate term at the London School of Economics, I started to wear the hijab. I was 23 and I had never worn it before. Whenever I prayed, I put special prayer clothes on top of my ordinary ones — a plain cotton skirt with a loose elasticated waist and a matching billowing veil which I pushed my head through — but I had never covered my hair in public. Neither did my friends, neither did my mother nor her friends nor my cousins. We did not think of ourselves as lesser Muslims for doing so. Instead we thought of ourselves as city people, modern and, to some extent, westernized. Yet it was only in the West, ten days after I arrived from Sudan, with my 1-year-old son, to start an MSc in Statistics, that I started to wear the hijab. I have been wearing it ever since — 35 years — most of which I've spent in Britain witnessing the evolving perceptions of Islam and its most visible marker, the hijab.

At the University of Khartoum, where I had been studying for my first degree before I came to London, many girls wore national dress — the tobe — which covered their hair and arms and a growing number did wear the hijab. I wore what was described as *moda*, an Arabized version of the French word for fashion. This meant Western/Egyptian clothes — skirts, blouses etc. with no head covering. Girls made up a quarter or perhaps a third of the student body. A good number of them dressed like me, "went *moda*," as it was described at the time, but still we were a minority within a minority. Naturally we were drawn to each other. Throughout my university years, I was friendly with girls who covered their hair in a variety of ways but my circle of close friends dressed as I did.

To cover or not cover and in general the position of women in Islam was a topic of heated discussion among students in forums and gatherings. The textual evidence — from the Qur'an and the Hadith — was presented and argued over. Both male and female students took part in this. We were attending the country's top university and we took ourselves seriously. From a religious point of view, we were also well-read. Islamic Studies, one of my favourite subjects, had been part of the school curriculum, the syllabus expansive and impressive. Our discussions were heated but not emotional; the emphasis was on logic rather than spirituality and they were an opportunity to showcase one's breadth of reading and how much could be quoted from memory. The principle that the hijab was solely a women's issue, for women alone to decide, would have been alien to us. Male scholars interpreting the Qur'an was the norm and it was not challenged. Strong, outspoken women throughout Islam's history had often, and still do, taken men to task for not obeying Allah's words, so the opposite was more than expected. Besides, many of the progressive issues regarding women — education, employment, the abolishment of FGM — were spearheaded by progressive men. How a woman dressed, whether modestly or not, veiled or not, was seen as an issue that mattered to men too.

I was convinced by the religious argument for wearing the hijab and I liked the look of it — romantic, old-fashioned, a bit mysterious. I gazed at the hijabi girls in the university, how they walked like princesses, the flow and grace of their clothes, their air of mystery and self-worth. They were hiding something valuable and precious, claiming their own space, their own confidence in their beauty. But still I did not take the step. It felt too drastic, a private need to come closer to Allah turning itself into a social statement. Would it suit me or not, I also wondered. Throughout my university years in Khartoum, the hijab became a future resolution among many others, an act of self-improvement that lay in the future. In the same way that I thought, one day I will go on hajj, one day I will fast more days than Ramadan, I also thought, one day I will wear the hijab but not yet. I did though adjust my wardrobe in that direction. I stopped wearing short sleeves or short skirts. I stopped wearing tight trousers. I was conscious of how I dressed. If covering my hair was too drastic a step, then I could concentrate on the modesty of my clothes. This worked in the sense that I was not making a statement and hardly anyone noticed. I continued to mull on the hijab and I certainly spoke about it a lot, to my friends who discouraged me, to my fiancé who mildly encouraged me but didn't seem to think I would ever take the plunge, to my father who disapproved, and to my mother who was neutral.

My friends discouraged me because they were liberal and left-leaning, they saw the hijab as regressive and a hindering of women's progress. A memory of that time illustrates this. I am walking alone out of a lecture and a male student I have never noticed before says he would like to have a word. He tells me that I am beautiful, that he's never seen a more beautiful girl in his life. If he hadn't been so serious, if his tone hadn't been so sombre, I would have burst out laughing. He says that this beauty puts on me the responsibility to wear the hijab. He says he is advising me to do so. Finally, there is a pause and I can speak. I say with deliberate coolness, thank you, and turn away. He is stumped. Surely he wants an argument, the chance to engage. I leave him and walk away as fast as possible. In the halls, I tell this story to my friends. They are incandescent. "How dare he speak to you like that?" they shout. "How dare he! Oh if I was there I would have roasted him, I would have wrung him, I would have torn him to shreds." They are livid and burning with indignation. "If anyone dares to come up to me and tell me how to dress," they add for good measure, "I'll show them!" It is their fondness for me that stops them from scorning my passive response, from telling me off. They believe they should have been there to protect me. I am amused, secretly proud that I had reacted with dignity. I had, in my own way, stopped him in his tracks. I had, in my own, shut him up. But my friends would have preferred a good fight, onlookers gathering while they put that young man firmly in his place. They knew too that I was leaning towards wearing the hijab. But they were confident that they could nip any such weakening on my part in the bud. If I did actually start wearing the hijab, they would talk me out of it in a few hours.

My fiancé took the opposite view. He encouraged me because he believed the hijab would protect me from harassment. Harassment was a word that we did not use then but was a daily fact of Sudanese public life. Like every young woman who had grown up in Khartoum, I had been trained to cope with the staring, catcalling, and occasionally worse by avoiding, shrugging off or repelling as appropriate. However, I had not been trained to cope with the kind of male attention I received years later when I first arrived in London. I assumed that Western men were friendlier and less inhibited, but I often misread situations and was unable to gauge the extent or nature of their interest. I was living in London without my husband, who was working at the time in the Middle East, and I found myself often confused and vulnerable. It is now a commonly held belief that how a woman dresses should not be a factor in how men behave towards her. If she is a victim of unwanted attention, she must not be blamed for how she dresses. Personally, though, I witnessed a strong and significant change in men's behaviour towards me as soon as I started wearing the hijab. Bus conductors became less friendly, acquaintances were less likely to express avid interest in Sudan; there were hardly any more offers to help me manoeuver my baby's pushchair. And most dramatic of all, the heckling from builders working high up on scaffoldings stopped completely. Now, this was London in 1987 when the word "Muslim" was hardly ever used, let alone recognized as an identity symbolized by the hijab. These London men were not reacting to an understanding of the hijab, it meant nothing to them. Instead, the toning down of the attention they paid me was an instinctive response to seeing less of my body.

Many years later, I was speaking about this experience to a young Muslim who had lived all her life in the UK and did not wear the hijab. She explained to me that there were specific modern/Western/British ways of rebuffing men's unwanted interests that I had not learnt growing up in Sudan. True, I knew how to protect myself from the crude harassments of the African street, but I had not learnt the more sophisticated methods. These, she explained, included reading a book when eating out alone, always talking about how happily married you were or at least mentioning your husband soon after introductions, not laughing too heartily at men's jokes, not asking them personal questions — clothes had nothing to do with it. This was a revelation for me. Perhaps that was why British women had photos of their partners and children in their offices. Perhaps that was why they tended to act cold. From a Muslim perspective, a woman's restrained behaviour with men was an integral part of the equation but the visual aspect, the clothes, had always been the definitive emphasis.

My father disapproved of the hijab because he saw it as ugly and old-fashioned. He was conservative in many ways and certainly supported modesty but to him the hijab symbolized a cultural past he wanted to shrug off. He had grown up in Umdurman at a time when women were house-bound and deprived of education and he did not want this kind of life for his daughter. Modernity, to him, was tied to Western dress, the aesthetics of the veil never appealed to him. It did though to me, and strongly so. I had grown up reading *Little Women* and *Jane Eyre* — all these long skirts and pinafores seemed to me romantic. Pictures of the Virgin Mary, Orientalist paintings of veiled women, the costumes in films like *Gone with the Wind* and *Doctor Zhivago*, these were my idea of beauty. When I started to wear the hijab my father grumbled but soon resigned himself to the idea. I have a sweet memory of him on a visit to London pleading with me that if I am insistent on covering my hair then I should use a casual veil like Benazir Bhutto did. She was much in the news at the time and we all admired her elegance. I wasn't convinced, though, that she was wearing a proper hijab.

"I dress as I please," I often hear women say, or "Women should be free to dress as they want." But how much freedom do we really have? In reality we wear what we can find affordable in the shops. I might love the clothes in *Crouching Tiger, Hidden Dragon*, but I doubt I can find or wear traditional Chinese clothes in the streets of Britain or Sudan. There are dynamics, practicalities, and conventions that effect what we wear and not all of them are about how much skin is revealed. Globalization has resulted in a greater uniformity of dress. National/traditional dress, which often includes a head covering for men as well as women, is in retreat. It is often more expensive and seen to be less practical. The growing norm is Western dress characterised by women revealing more skin and contours than men. In bitter winters, brave leading ladies walk down red carpets in gorgeous evening gowns that expose a good part of their upper bodies to the elements. Next to them, the leading men are snug in their woollen suits. This is the norm, rarely challenged and increasingly adopted by non-Western societies.

I recall an incidence that took place in the LSE a few months after I started wearing the hijab. I was sharing the lift with a student I did not know. When she spoke I realized she was American. "Why do you dress like that?" she asked. Along with my headscarf, I was wearing a jumper and an ankle length skirt. Startled, I could not think of a quick reply. As if backtracking she said, "I suppose how I dress is odd to you too." She was wearing jeans and a sweatshirt; she did not look odd to me at all. Cultural relativity is convincing in abstract terms. In reality, cultures are not equidistant from each other. Throughout the world, the hegemony of Western clothes for men and women has found little resistance. Perhaps the hijab is the only resistance, it comes across as "political," the symbol of an identity at odds with Western values. But from a religious point of view, this position of defiance can be highly problematic.

Religious compliance is a form of worship. Worship must be sincere and solely for the sake of the Almighty. It should not be done in the spirit of rebellion. It should neither be about scoring a point nor asserting a position nor taking a stand. Worship is about humility, not pride. It is about hope in acceptance, not arrogance in running against the tide. It was my mother who taught me this. In the long years in which I discussed with her the option of wearing the hijab, she neither encouraged nor discouraged me.

My mother was neutral because, being devout, she understood instinctively what took me longer to understand — that the hijab dilemma was superficial, a red herring, a very small step in the arduous climb to spiritual fulfilment. A change that would by no means be sufficient. It is more difficult to forgive, lower our pride, give unconditional love, curb envy, help the needy than it is to adopt a dress code. It is more difficult to pray with focus day in and day out, to be grateful, to fight our own indulgences, to discipline our egos than it is to lower a hem or wrap a scarf. Vanity, selfishness, blind ambition and greed — battling against them is harder than swapping fashions.

Those who opposed the hijab, because they were afraid it would limit women's progress, were chasing the wrong culprit. Women's advancement in Sudan and much of the Muslim world continued parallel to the widespread popularity of the hijab. The Sudanese street (before the recent war) was completely different than what it had been in the 1980s with more women driving, walking, and heading to work. Unlike in my days, women were half the student body, sometimes even more. This trend can be found in other Muslim countries too. Muslim women have always had rights of property ownership, but now they are active in business forums, the real estate industry and the stock exchange. In their personal lives too, things have been improving. Polygamy is on the decline. Divorce, which has always been allowed and catered for by the Sharia, has become easier and more socially acceptable. It is still the norm for single women to live with their families, but seeking work or education in another city is now a legitimate reason for leaving home. Divorced and widowed women have started to defy society and live alone. Although patriarchal pressure is still strong on the young, women over 40 have considerably more clout and leeway to live as they please. Muslim women now are also quicker and more assertive in holding men to account. Society tends to indulge male indiscretions, but one of the results of greater education for women is that they now refuse to turn a blind eye and insist assertively that if religious prohibitions apply to them then they must equally apply to their brothers and husbands too. This trajectory of greater empowerment and equality (slow but steady) has been done with the hijab and not without it.

In my time at the LSE, I once attended a talk held by the Islamic Society. Whether the topic was women and the hijab or whether the discussion led to that, I am not sure. I remember the speaker, a soft-spoken scholar, hapless at the onslaught of objections to the hijab that came from the mainly Pakistani women in the audience. "But how can I play tennis," one of them cried out. In 1987, deciding to wear the hijab meant giving up most sports and definitely swimming. The burkini was yet to be invented and modest sport clothes were still a thing of the future. I was never sporty, so for me the hijab was a relief more than a restriction. For many other women, though, it was a considerable sacrifice. And it is to the credit of younger women who were innovative and pioneering that nowadays there is a growing number of Muslim sportswomen who wear the hijab. And outside the world of sports, in the police, on oil rigs, laboratories, boardrooms and cockpits it has also been possible to accommodate the hijab.

Despite years of mulling it over, the first time I actually started to wear the hijab was the result of a sudden decision. I had gone to bed the night before without even thinking about it. There was so much else to think about, so much newness. My baby, just over 1 year, had only ever lived in Sudan. Here, he had to be in new clothes, woollen jumpers and socks, necessary for the cold. The pushchair needed a cover for the rain, even certain items of food were different. The novelty of taking him to the park, the newness of duvets and radiators. My mother was with me, helping to look after him while I went to lectures, but she was on sabbatical leave doing her own research and in those early weeks in London, I was busy looking for extra childcare. The start of the academic year was harsh. I had missed the orientation and was floundering. The course was difficult, I was out of my depth and I knew it. Anxiety gnawed at me and I missed my husband who was working miles away, and in those years before Skype and WhatsApp, our expensive long distance phone calls were too brief and occasional.

That morning in October, I woke up from a nightmare of wandering down a path in which thorny bushes were closing in on me. With relief, my baby's babbling voice greeted me. I picked him up from his cot, kissed him and enjoyed the feel of his fleece sleepsuit against my skin. But I had to leave him. The rushed breakfast, the need to hurry so as not to miss the bus. On my way out, I grabbed a scarf, any scarf it would seem. This one was white cotton and I wrapped it around my head. Not wanting my mother to see me, I shouted goodbye and dashed out of the flat and into the cold sunshine of the street.

London in 1987, where the word "Muslim" was hardly used, where women in hijabs were few and far between. No one knew me here, no one would judge, no one would care. I felt all alone, an individual soul. Even in the university I had yet to make friends. No one commented, perhaps no one noticed. A rush around me of classes and assignments, a canteen lunch I was still not used to, losing myself in corridors. On the way home I caught a glimpse of myself in a shop window. I did not like what I saw — the look wasn't right, the colours unmatched — but it was already too late, I had taken the plunge, grabbed an opportunity, and fulfilled a resolution that had been germinating for a long time. Here, I was in a city where I was free and this was how I was choosing to use this freedom.

These were hardly the best circumstances in which to make a wardrobe change. I had no time for shopping. Studying and looking after my baby and navigating a new life, I had no choice but to take the hijab in my stride. Eventually I learnt to coordinate colours and to figure out the best place to buy scarves. Eventually a look evolved which suited me and felt comfortable at the same time. But those early days were the most difficult. I remember meeting on the bus an elderly Palestinian woman to whom I blurted out that I was finding it difficult to wear the hijab. Difficult in the sense that I did not like what I saw in the mirror. She gently encouraged me and I felt better after talking to her.

Bonnets, hats, the veils that nuns wore — from novels and period dramas, I had thought these to be Western and underestimated how the hijab in Europe would be perceived as alien, unconnected to Victorian modesty or Christian teaching. It is assumed that the hijab is specifically Islamic and a product of the here and now. Overlaps with other religions and previous eras are played down if not ignored. Yet the concept of women's modesty is widespread throughout the world — it takes different forms and fashions. When I meet middle-aged practicing Christian women, I notice how they neither dye their hair nor tidy their eyebrows nor use makeup. It is their way of fighting vanity and, in my opinion, stricter than the hijab which conceals the "faults" of ageing and gives a more flattering look.

Of all the things I could have done to improve myself spiritually, the hijab had not been the easiest but then neither was it the most difficult. It has been though, without doubt, the most visible, affecting how others see me and how they react. Maybe without it I would have had better career prospects or more friends, but these gains would have been superficial. With maturity comes less care for other people's approval. With maturity comes the understanding that the fairer verdict is arrived at when we are our own judge, accountable for our own actions.

I have never felt restricted by the hijab. Often I forget that I am wearing it. It is just how I dress, how I've always dressed for the past 35 years, another item of clothing. When I was younger, it protected me. Now it makes it easier for me to accept the changes that come with age. It was a privilege to start wearing it at a time when it had no meaning to the majority of the people around me, no symbol or definition. A private choice, mine alone, connected to my personal faith, what had always been there from the beginning. For I don't remember finding out that Allah Almighty existed in the same way that I don't remember finding out my name. I know that in addition to being a woman, I am a human soul in need of spiritual nourishment and access to the Divine. Clothes are but one way, out of thousands, that can make the spiritual journey easier and faster.

identity is a territory
Olja Alvir

Poetry

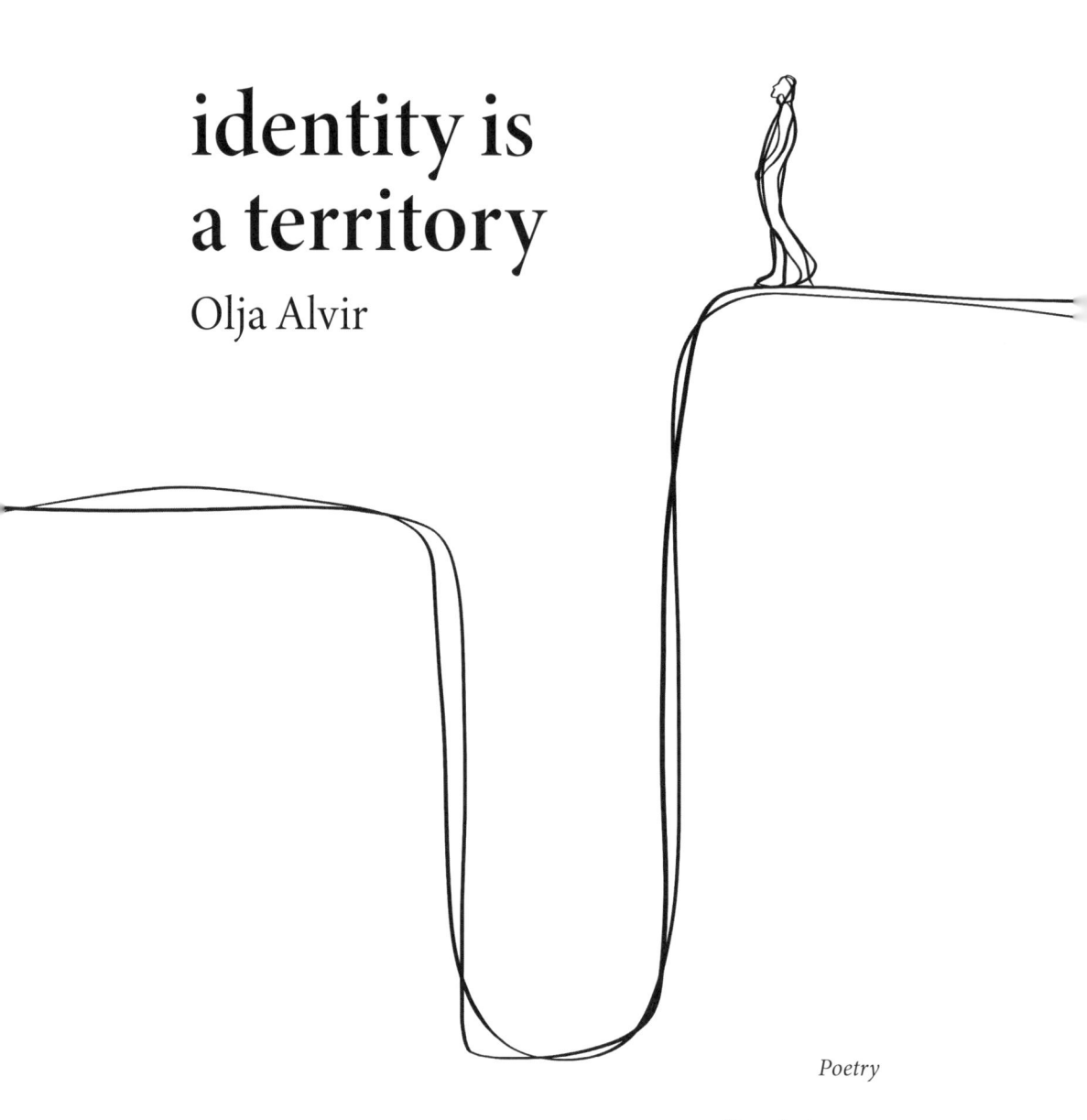

NATIONALITY   Yugoslaviennese
FIRST LANGUAGES   Serbocroatian & German
SECOND LANGUAGES   English & French

Appeared in Issue Spring '22

identity is a territory
ever striving to describe the sea
its roots in all the wrong places.

on this plateau i am not lost
though, i'm just a visitor
traveling at the speed of causality

or a stranger, thank you
i'd like to keep it that way.
driftwood on this wasted mesa

maybe a cat that comes back after a year
carrying the what ifs of unwanted adulthood:
between con and artist.

i know that we can't upend the earth and
hold ourselves hostage among its crevices
but i can't deny that i feel it too:

tectonic temptations, the
sweet, sweet calling of forever,
of things decided and done.

there's no place against home

A Brief Chronology of My English Accent

Tim Tim Cheng

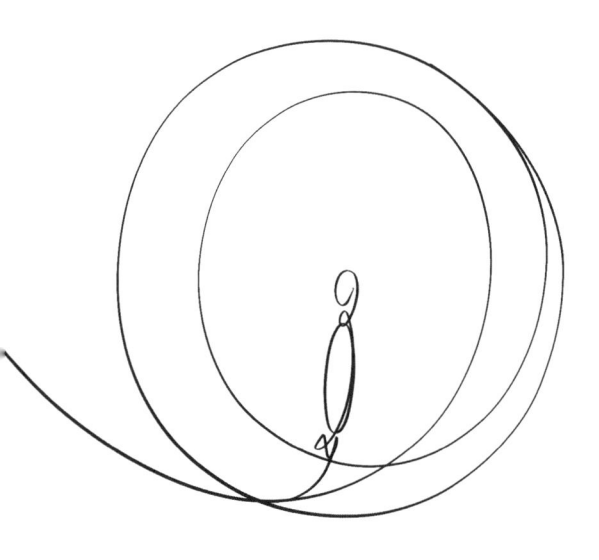

Poetry

NATIONALITY   Chinese (Hong Kong)
FIRST LANGUAGE   Cantonese
SECOND LANGUAGES   English & Mandarin

Appeared in Issue Fall '21

1993 — Wailing inside the NICU was my first language.

1996 — The first word came during kindergarten, a cloudburst of Cantonese breaking the hidden Hokkien bank.

1997 — Migration lends me names: *Tin Tin* in Hokkien, *Tian Tian* in Mandarin, and *Tim Tim* in British Hong Kong. The character for my name, 恬, equates 'being quiet' to 'sweetness', carrying my mother's humble blessing.

2005–2008 — A history teacher we loved read Croatia as *Co-tee-ah*. Some teachers used more English words when they were angry. Every syllable punched, heavy as a single Chinese character. I do this too to make myself clear.

2009 — A sky full of songs blanketed me. I took *South London* from Florence + the Machine on YouTube and The Horrors in NME.

2013 — University poetry courses taught us to dissect our name's radicals. I found a *heart next to a tongue, a tongue* made of a *thousand mouths*. My name is the sound of *licking* the *sky shamelessly*.

2014 — My name is *Tim Tam* in Australia, *Dim Dim* outside an Estonian bar, *Chin Chin* for drunk French exchange students.

2015 — My accent is a passport full of travel stamps. My accent is the peeling bark of a tree I hugged in Brisbane. My accent snowed Estonian ice crystals in the ears of an American in Vietnam.

2016 — A British teacher I worked with remarked that my accent was beautiful. I didn't know compliments could hurt.

2017 — My accent is also the way Phoebe sings "Smelly Cat."

2019 — My accent almost gave me a pay raise. My boss thought I was "almost native."

2021 — I am longing for a new country to grow on my tongue. The way 'aspire' and 'aspirate' share the same noun.

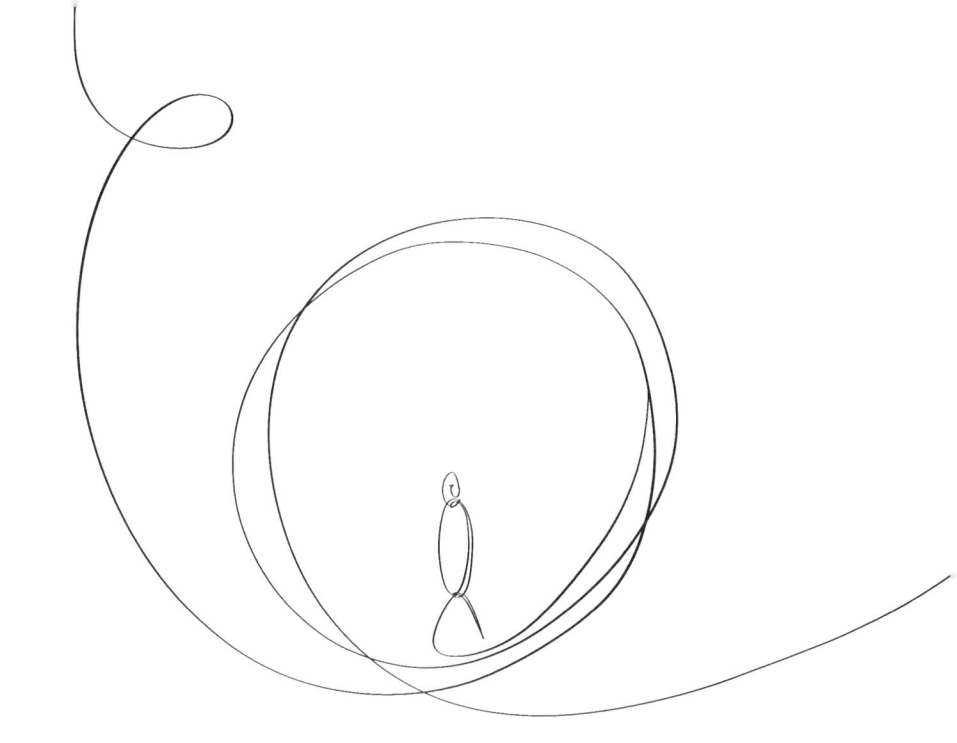

An Ode to My Inner Ballerina

Brianna Colmenares

Poetry

NATIONALITY Puerto Rican & Dominican
FIRST LANGUAGE Spanish
SECOND LANGUAGE English

Appeared in Issue Spring '22

I am Clara, I am Alice
running circles in my pointe shoes
the Dodo, and the Dormouse stare.
The March Hare hounds her to stop.
He is dizzy. Tweedledee and Tweedledum find me as
I am on the way to the Kingdom
of Snow begging me to show them how to calypso.
In a perfect world the Queen of Hearts and
the Rat King will wed and I will
be left alone to leap all over Wonderland.

In a world of my
own I would simply sissone
over the flowers singing "Golden Afternoon."
Twirl in between the changing hues of the caterpillar's
hookah smoke. I would trade my itty bitty
mushroom piece for
one of those Christmas
cookies. I would remain the size
of grass — three inches tall. If only
to stay in my head.

Coty 24
Jee Ann Guibone

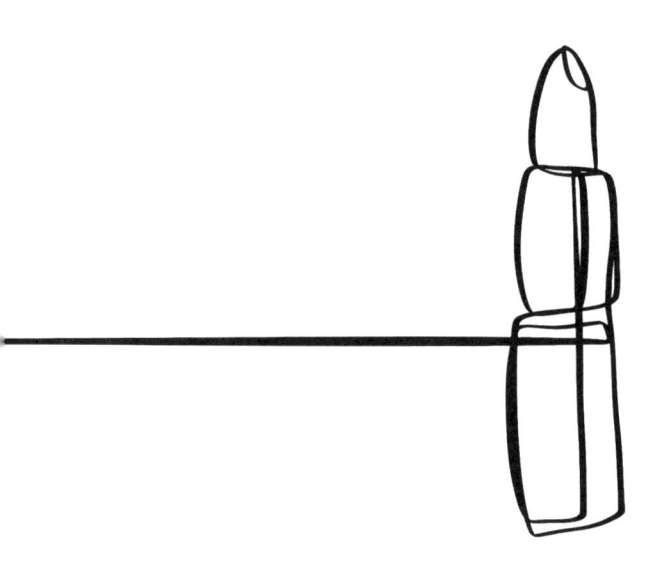

Fiction

NATIONALITY   Filipino
FIRST LANGUAGE   Cebuano/Bisaya
SECOND LANGUAGES   English & Tagalog

Appeared in Issue Spring '23

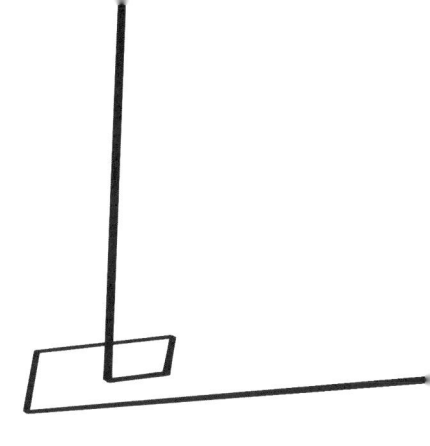

"Your mother looks hideous."

I absolutely agree, except I don't say it out loud because you're probably listening in right now, your spirit floating in the house, judging us like you always do.

"Wipe her face," Tita Angela continues, knocking my elbow. "You have that fancy Korean makeup, right? With this storm, the *manalabtan* won't be here till 9. You've got time."

Never mind the prayer leader, I think, looking out the window to see the backyard all but flooded. The palm trees loom tall around the property like sentinels, slightly bowed but still standing. *Nobody's* coming tonight, what with the storm.

I wonder if this house is going to get blown off in the storm. This is, what, a hundred years old? Probably older. I remember we used to have leaks in the ceiling. We put every bucket and pail we owned in the living room and kitchen to catch the rain. And then we used them to water the plants and flush the toilet.

God, the toilet — the outhouse, I mean. Every night nature called, I felt like I was doing an obstacle course: climb over you and the old man, step over Ray and Cynthia, tiptoe across the living room, open the door to the patio, clamber down the steps twice the length of my skinny 10-year-old legs and run through the *silong*.

Every time, I looked up through the spaces between the wooden floorboards and watched out for your footsteps, heart hammering in my chest.

And inside the outhouse, the sole source of light was the moon. It filtered through the slits separating the walls and the corrugated tin roof.

The only thing we could afford to turn into concrete were the walls around the toilet; paint was a luxury, so everything was brown and gray.

When I tell Tita Angela I didn't bring my fancy-shmancy makeup kit with me, she gives me a disbelieving look. You know the one, where she throws her right shoulder back, raises her pencil-thin eyebrows high, and presses her chin down against her neck. Your sister is as dramatic as you; thankfully, not as loud or confrontational.

You, meanwhile, had threatened a full-grown man twice your size for short-changing you even a single peso.

A roll of thunder shakes the weak foundations of this ancient house, and the young boys try to see who can scream the loudest. Tita Angela silences them with a single "*Saba!*" and raises one rubber slipper in warning.

The teenagers check their phones, and one of them, 15-year-old Shayna Lynn, announces that there's no signal. Tito Dodong slaps his thighs and wonders aloud if we should postpone the *novena*.

You would have said no. You would have knocked the back of his head and told him to exchange his basketball shorts for khakis and his faded *Buffalo Soldier* T-shirt with the fraying sleeves for a plain polo shirt.

I half expect you to open the casket and stand up, demand that the prayers start. *Who are we waiting for?* you would say. *The archbishop? The Pope?* And you would turn to me and say, *Stephanie, what are you standing there for? Get my prayer book. Useless! You're useless! Every single one of you!*

You with your face in clown makeup.

I chuckle.

I'm sorry, I can't help it. You really do look ridiculous — not that it's a surprise. Funeral packages are not known for the "natural" makeup look.

Maybe I should just leave you like that, looking like Pennywise the murdering alien clown. Do you know Pennywise? I bet you don't. You hated horror movies. Or maybe you know now. Do dead people acquire world knowledge upon death? Posthumous wisdom-osmosis?

Will you haunt me if I don't fix your face?

Not like it'll make a difference. You've been haunting me since the day I left.

I get Ray and 17-year-old Jasper to take off the glass cover. I take a wooden stool from the dining room and sit beside your casket fashioned with elegant silver interiors and handles — the casket that I paid for, by the way. Not because I wanted to. I hope you know that, if it were up to me, you would be buried in flimsy cardboard.

But through emotional manipulation, Tita Angela guilted me into getting you a better-looking casket.

"What will the neighbors and relatives say when they see your *Nanay* buried in a cheap coffin? Her eldest daughter works as a *fashionista* in Spain, but she can't afford to give her mother a nice burial?"

She had a lot of nerve trying to take me on a guilt-trip. Tita was there when you threw my things into the sidewalk. When you ripped my diary the minute you found out I had a girlfriend. When you threw me out of your life.

She was just *there*, standing in the *silong*, one hand clutching the front of her flower-patterned duster dress and another wrapped around her young son's shoulders.

I still remember how Lola Maming backed you up, standing at the top of the stairs, encouraging you like a devil on your shoulder, this old woman who never missed mass, prayed the rosary every afternoon, and read the Bible cover to cover.

You were banshees, both of you, screeching that mid-afternoon, bony fingers pointing at me, casting a hex on my life, calling for my death.

You knew why I never came home for her funeral. You *knew*. Yet you told everyone who would listen that I was ungrateful, rebellious, head so big with my own achievements that I had floated up to the sky like a balloon.

You weren't far off. Leaving you, leaving this place, *was* like floating in the sky. You weren't there to hold me down — no *Useless! Stupid! Lazy!* to wrap around my ankles like chains, no *Ingrate! Heretic! Devil!* to circle my neck like a leash.

You were my shackles, mother dear. And the day you threw me out was the day I became free.

That was, perhaps, the greatest gift you had given me.

But now I'm back in this house after so many decades. You have a bathroom inside the house now, thank god. The floorboards seem new, cherry-red and smooth, recently varnished. Looks like you made use of your nephews and nieces, not to mention Ray and Cynthia, one a civil engineer and the other a public school teacher.

They're weird around me, Cynthia overly polite and Ray awkward like a teenager, unable to meet my eyes. They don't know me.

Oh, they remember their 19-year-old big sister carrying a backpack and a woven plastic bag filled with everything she owned under the sun as she walked away from the only home she had ever known. They remember me sharing a box of Curly Tops chocolates with them. They remember us fighting over the last cheese-filled *puto* during fiesta. But they don't know me.

They don't know that I landed in Spain on a scholarship and worked two jobs for rent and food. They don't know that my girlfriend broke up with me because I befriended the liquor store.

My only siblings don't know that I crawled my way out of the bottles of pills and spirits to pull myself together — and still I feel like a weathered old T-shirt, washed out, threads unraveling at the seams, filled with holes. Or maybe I'm an old jigsaw puzzle with missing pieces and corners bent and scorched by careless hands, the rough passing of years, and the memory of an old woman's bitter anger.

No one in this house knows who I am. You made sure of that.

Yet here I am, on special request.

"Your mother wanted to see you, you know," Tita Angela had said, that arsonist who spreads guilt instead of fire, watching avidly as filial obligation and societal pressure licked at my heels like flames. "Before she died, she told me to find you and ask you to come home."

Did you really? Did you want me to come home? Or did she only say that so she and everyone else can feast on me like vultures? They circle around, watch my every move, and whisper when they think I can't hear them.

Even now as I wipe your face, I can feel eyes on me.

Your skin feels so strange. It's a little rubbery, a little soft. I wipe the lipstick off first. It's a dark red, something you would never wear. Come to think of it, I don't know how you look with makeup. I don't remember an instance when you so much as wore lipstick. The closest you got was a swipe of lip gloss for my grade school graduation.

Next to go is the powder that sits on your face like a sheet of paper, too white and obvious. Tita Angela was right. Your visitors will take one look at you and murmur about your makeup. It will be the highlight of their evening — second only to the news of your prodigal lesbian daughter coming home to pay her respects, of course.

Now that all the makeup is gone, I take out Tita's BB cream and spread it on your face. We never got to do this, did we? You never taught me how to do my hair or wear makeup. I learned the first one from my first-grade teacher and the second one from the gays at the salon next to my high school.

What are you going to do with makeup? you once said. *Don't be a slut. You don't need that to get good grades. Focus on your studies.*

I push a bead of cream across your cheeks and stretch the skin a little bit, my hands itching to pinch, to hurt. You're already dead anyway. You don't care, do you?

Then I take a deep breath and spread the cream evenly.

You know, I think this is our first mother–daughter bonding experience without the insults and physical pain. Isn't that funny?

I press, setting powder on your face and move on quickly to your eyebrows. They were always so sparse, like scattered bamboo trees. They made you look like a witch, I secretly thought, especially when you talked in a high, reedy voice.

What color should I use on your brows then?

Ash or gray to match my hair.

The closest shade in Tita's palette is an ash brown. I paint your brows softly, the hairs responding so gently that, for a moment, I forget you're a corpse, cold and silent, unable to scream and hurt.

Eye shadow?

A natural shade. Maybe light brown, a little rose pink?

I'm impressed. You've got good taste!

I blend the shades and lean back to admire my work. Can you see yourself? I did a better job than the one from the funeral parlor, right? Even you can admit that. Tell me I did a good job.

You did. You are very talented, Stephanie.

The blush and bronzer are next. I mean, sure, everyone knows you're dead, but you don't have to *look* dead. The bronzer gives your face a soft definition. I blend it in and marvel at your jaw. Obviously, it's stiff now, trapped shut with wire, or so I read on Google.

Nanay, why did you hate me so much?

Hm?

Oh, *now* you're quiet. Now, you're giving me the silent treatment after you've been haunting me all these years.

"Wow, you're good," Cynthia says, appearing over my shoulder. Her long dark hair swings like that bead curtain framing the door to the dining room. "She doesn't look like a clown now."

I giggle and turn to her. If she's gonna be buried with makeup, she should at least look good, I say.

Cynthia gives me a considering look, her eyes soft, her lips frozen in a disappearing smile. Her face is tanned and smooth, no pimple in sight. She's 27 now, a fully functioning adult, with a policeman boyfriend I've only seen in her Facebook photos.

"Do you have your own salon in Madrid?" she asks, turning back to look at your immobile face.

No, I say. I tell her that I'm actually a fashion designer. I run a small boutique that specializes in wedding attire and jewelry. My designs have been featured in Spanish movies and TV shows.

"Wow," Cynthia says again and wrenches her eyes away from you. She leans casually against your casket. "I'd love to visit you. I've never been abroad."

Just tell me when, I say. I'll give you a tour.

And her smile is wide.

Because she can, if she wants. She's free now. You can't stop her. You can't disown her or humiliate her for not doing what you want.

"What lipstick are you gonna use?" she asks.

I sift through the expired makeup in Tita Angela's bag ("Take these, so that I can finally throw them out after you use them.") but come up short. There's no lipstick.

"Maybe there's one in Nanay's room."

I doubt that, and I tell her so.

She shrugs. "Well, you never know. She might have been hoarding makeup since the 70s."

We both chuckle, the tension of being in each other's unfamiliar space softening.

"The *manalabtan* just texted!" Tita Angela shouts into the living room. "She'll be here in 30 minutes. Cynthia, find your mother's prayer book!"

I'll do it, I say, standing up. Hopefully there *is* a hoard of vintage makeup in your room.

I climb upstairs. There's only one long fluorescent bulb in the middle of the space. It's right outside the room you and the old man once shared before he died.

Bad liver, drank too much, Tita Angela, the family historian, told me.

I step into your former space and flick the switch on. There's only one light in the middle of the ceiling, and it casts everything in yellow. The walls are made of thin wood. The timber columns haven't been replaced since I last saw them. The foundations of this house have remained the same.

But there are marks of change. The toilet, the new furniture, the beaded curtains. Those must have been your decision. Nothing happens in this house without your say-so.

But now you're gone. What does that mean for everyone?

Your bed takes up most of the space, pushed to the left for the altar on the right. A Santo Niño holds court in the middle of the table. Behind it is a framed illustration of the Sacred Heart of Jesus, the Christ looking like a white European model. A small statue of Our Lady of Perpetual Help stands next to it. There's a bunch of rosaries tangled together over some prayer booklets.

And beside them is a tin box that used to contain biscuits. Curious, I open it, fully expecting a sewing kit. Instead, what I find are folded pieces of paper. They're yellow and smudged brown, the blue ink bleeding through the back of the paper. And in the corner of the box is a lipstick.

It's a Coty 24.

A loud slap echoes in the room. I jump, throwing the lipstick back into your box.

Another hit, flesh against flesh, rings next to my ear, and I turn around.

And I see you.

Words are being thrown around, but they're garbled like you're underwater. No, *I'm* underwater. I'm… peeking in from behind the door. I'm watching and listening, immobile, frozen.

The old man is hitting your head, holding your arm. The lipstick sits on the altar. He points at it, grabs it, and throws it against the wall. It breaks in two.

He shoves you against the Sto. Niño. A small statue of a crucified Christ tumbles and shatters. When he turns toward the door, I unstuck myself, stumble backwards, and run. I leave you behind.

The memory fades as quickly as it appeared.

I turn back to the lipstick and cradle it in my hands. I can see it now, the jagged lines where you had smeared Rugby glue to repair it. I pull at the ends, but there's no give. You patched it up really well.

A Coty 24. A real vintage find, this one. I take off the cap. The lipstick hasn't been used at all. It looks new, the creamy pink color a little off but the texture still smooth.

I look at the folded pieces of paper and open them one by one.

Dear Celia.

I haven't heard your name in a long time. I mean, you were never "Celia" to me. You were "Nanay." And after I left, you were someone I dared not name.

I scan the bottom of the letter and an unfamiliar name jumps at me. *Love, Bernadette.*

I open the other letters. *Love, Bernadette. Yours, Bernadette. Always and forever, Bernadette.* Bernadette, Bernadette, Bernadette.

A hollow kind of anger starts to consume me, like someone is taking a spoon to my chest, scooping out my heart and my ribs and all my insides. I feel so empty, a spacious cavern filled with nothing.

You betrayed me.

You — *you were like me.*

You could have been my greatest ally.

You could have protected me and supported me and loved me.

Instead, you saw in me everything you could have been but were afraid to be. And you drove me away. You threw me against the wall, watched me break, and left me to glue myself together.

Why won't you say anything now? Why aren't you talking?!

I throw your stupid box on the bed; I tear your letters in half and scatter them in the air.

What are you gonna do now? What are you gonna say?

You've haunted me all my life, but now you won't talk. Now, you're quiet. Now, you're distant. Now, you're *gone*!

My knees give way, and I fall on the altar, knocking the statuette over. I drop my head against the Sto. Niño. Hot tears press against my eyelids.

A strange warmth covers my shoulders like a shawl. Silver hair falls over my face. Calloused hands run over my cheeks, but my eyes remain closed.

When I do open them again, I'm alone.

But there's a piece of paper caught on the edge of the table. *Dear Stephanie*, it reads. I look around at the torn letters and begin the process of piecing them together.

"Where have you been?" Tita Angela shouts, grabbing my arm as soon as I step down from the stairs. "The *manalabtan* is here, as well as the neighbors! Clean up the casket while I hand out the coffee."

I walk over to you and take out the Coty 24. I apply it to your lips, whisper-like, just a touch of color. It doesn't slide as smoothly as I would have wanted, but it does the job. It coats your lips in a soft natural pink.

"Is it done?" Cynthia asks, standing beside me. She looks down, and her brows are raised. "That's amazing!" She lets out a soft sigh. "She looks beautiful."

I place an arm around her shoulders and lean in. "She does, doesn't she?"

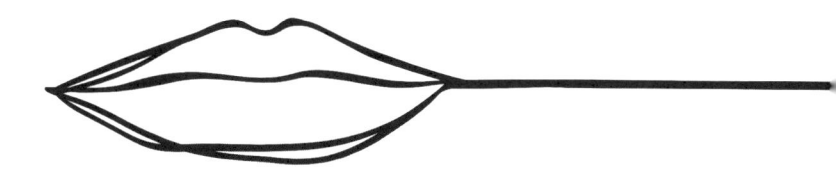

Can You See?
Thea Inuk Lønberg-Jensen

Flash Nonfiction

NATIONALITY Danish
FIRST LANGUAGE Danish
SECOND LANGUAGE English

Appeared in Issue Fall '21

"There's a man here who has changed his gender and he... erh, *she* says she has booked a test," the nurse said into the phone, her voice low and her eyes dutifully fixed on the computer screen on her desk. They only strayed briefly to look at me, averting themselves again as soon as they could.

I sit at a bus stop outside Hvidovre hospital. A bus rolls slowly by. Stops. Waits. Its engine humming rhythmically. I don't get on. I just stay on my bench, waiting for it to drive away.

A woman with a grey scarf sits on *my* bench, a lit cigarette in her hand, the smoke drifting lazily in the mild wind. Her chest barely covers the blue sign on the wall beside her depicting an x-ed out cigarette much like the one in her hand. She doesn't look at the sign or the many other signs around her. She chooses not to see, or maybe she is unable to? Maybe she has chosen not to look at those signs for so long, she is blind to them — forever in ignorance until some stranger dares to point out their existence to her, and then the woman has to admit to herself that they were there all along. A surprised "Oh..." and a "Sorry" if you're lucky.

A woman with a stroller walks past me on her way into the hospital. Two blue eyes above a blue facemask drift slightly my way, jump back to the entrance in front of her. Her heels click decidedly on the pavement, and the sound, intermingling with the humming of the bus, composes a short symphony before she reaches one of the big glass doors. Almost the entire front of the hospital is glass — both floors. Unnecessarily towering windows permitting anyone to look through as if to show you that this is, in fact, a hospital. A hospital performing itself, the performance barely dimmed by a couple of curtains drawn on the top floor. Just to be safe, a big sign above the doors exclaims the obvious: "Hvidovre Hospital."

I had come to the hospital to get a blood test. I had been here before, many times in fact, but this time was different. I had scanned my card, waited in line, talked to the woman at the reception. But the system was not prepared, and they couldn't see me. I never had my test, because it wasn't for me. It was for someone who is here but who doesn't exist anymore. At least not officially.

The next bus rolls slowly by. Stops. Waits. People get out and walk towards the glass entrance, the patients inside so clearly visible from the outside. I wonder why some of the curtains are drawn. I wonder if someone has forgotten to pull them aside and let the light and the sight in. Are all the curtains closed at night? Probably not, but if they were, wouldn't people get confused? If there was no performance to watch, they would have to just trust that sign above the glass doors. Trust what the hospital is telling them despite not being able to see for themselves. I can't imagine them not being confused, because that is what they always are when I show them my sign.

I had left the blood test department, wandered into the nearest bathroom. I called my doctor, but the line was closed for the day. I sat down on the floor, too low for the mirror above the sink to tell me what I already knew. My eyes stung, and I wiped them off with the toilet paper beside me, careful not to smear my mascara. Then I got up, ignored the mirror, left the bathroom, kept walking out through a big glass door, kept walking until I reached my bench.

A small tree stands beside the bus stop. Its bark is smooth and dark and its branches curl and twist in crude formations. There are no leaves on it, although a few buds do dress the crown. White and silky, they are almost in bloom. Tiny buds with flowers on the inside. I can't see the flowers yet, but I still know that they are there.

Another bus rolls slowly by. Stops. Waits. I get on.

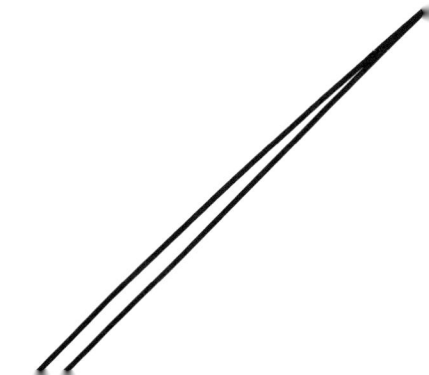

from Color(s) of the DAY
Yuko Otomo

Poetry

NATIONALITY Japanese & U.S.
FIRST LANGUAGE Japanese
SECOND LANGUAGE English

Previously unpublished

DAY ONE   (aug. 27, wed)

> Any color, so long as it's grey.
> — Samuel Beckett

The first color I was drawn to amongst all the colors of the phenomenal world in Paris was naturally & very appropriately GREY. "Paris Grey!" S & I simultaneously said to each other. Light shimmering through the variations of grey layered by ever-changing cloud formations, the city welcomed us back with the grey(s) all those painters had used through the ages.

    C kindly & lovingly came to pick us up. We walked to the airport's underground basement garage to find her car. The basement space was quiet with no one around. Sunflower yellow was painted like a band on the wall all over with sunflower images here & there. Soon I realized C was wearing the same sunflower colored narrow belt on her black outfit, carrying her big purse in the same sunflower yellow.

灰色 *hai-iro*   A grey sky.
曇り空 *kumori-zora*   A cloudy sky.
雲の向こう側の太陽 *kumo-no-muko-gawa no-taiyo*   The sun behind
                                                                                                                   the clouds.
向日葵 *himawari*   Sunflowers.
地下 *chika*/地上 *chijo*/空 *sora*   Underground/Aboveground/Sky.

from Color(s) of the DAY

DAY TWO   (aug. 28, thu)

Instead of picking the color(s) of the day, I let myself be picked by them. As we descended the spiral stairway, the tiny leaves of summer weeds in the planter by the window called me. Fragile & rather pale, this green color survived the cold summer.

緑色 *midori-iro*   Green.

Oh, I should not forget that the first color of the day was the non-color white which my eyes saw when I woke up in bed. White walls, a white ceiling — I still wonder why black & white & their combinations are considered as "non-colors." To my eyes, they *are* definitely colors, living in the family of color.

We met our old friend from NYC, who now lives in London, near Metro Pigalle as planned for lunch. She was on her way to Valencia to wash her stress away in the sun & in the water. We sat at our favorite café. I stretched out to see the sky. It was light blue with some white clouds patching parts.

空色 *sora-iro* Sky color.   青 *ao*   Blue.

In Japanese, my mother tongue, it is "sky color," not "blue color." I still remember the 空色 *sora-iro* Cray-Pas I loved using when I was a child.

青空 *ao-zora* Blue sky.

In English, we use "blue" not "sky." Simply complicated, or complicatedly simple. It's interesting how we use some narrative symbolic elements to indicate the tones & the types of color.

As I stretched toward the blue sky, I saw the blue awning of the bakery next door; sky color & blue color in one view. As I returned to the conversation at the table, my eyes caught a man's blue shirt. Then, a beggar with a dirty blue backpack. Also, a window cleaner with a mop, other tools & his bucket, which were also all blue.

A friend needed to take a train to Barcelona at Gare de Lyon. We decided to walk along Blvd. Magenta to check out the newly renovated Republic. Along the way, trees shone their last peak of green color. The season was changing in front of our eyes. So many painters had painted trees

& sky all through history. I kept thinking about them & their works as I walked toward Republic with *S* & *N*.

My eyes caught the color green shared by so many other things: big garbage bins waiting on the curb for the city sanitation trucks to empty out; traffic "GO" & a sign for a pharmacy…

But the most delicate green was the color of new sprouting leaves of trees along the boulevard, those cut down to stumps. A tree trunk with tree rings sprouting new, fresh leaves. They are almost unnoticeable, hiding behind the trunk. Transparent & shy, I wondered if they would survive the coming change of seasons.

DAY THREE   (aug. 29, fri)

茶色 *cha-iro*   Brown.   黄土色 *odo-iro*   Yellow ocher.

The tea color. Brown. Yellow earth color. Yellow ocher.
I saw quite a few fallen leaves already on the streets.

枯葉 *kare-ha*   Autumn leaves.

Dried & dead leaves. A song.

An old woman's cane which carries her solitude. The wooden bowls we eat the food from. The wicker basket where the bread rests. Part of the skin of a grilled fish I ate for lunch, which was closer to black but not quite, still brown. The surface of freshly baked bread is more like the color of falling leaves, but shinier. Clay flower pots & planters (on the window sill) are a quiet reddish brown. A boy's pants. A girl's boots. Both brown, being anxious for the new season. An old church's tile/brick walls. An old church's old wooden door & a wooden cross. An old piano left alone with an old wooden chair. The wooden handle of an old hammer.

All brown.

Meditating on the color brown in the many things I saw, I lay down on the ocher colored leather couch. My eyes were fixed on the white of the ceiling & soon I realized that the wooden floor was pale ocher, too.

木 *ki*   Tree.   樹 *ki*   Tree.   樹々 *kigi*   Trees.   森 *mori*   Forest.
土 *tsuchi*   Earth.   水 *mizu*   Water.   空 *sora*   Sky.

Amazingly, most things made of wood have the color brown or ocher: the color of the earth.

sunset

the sun
disappears
behind
the houses
on the hill

trees
in an empty park
lose
their colors
to become

影絵 *kage-e*   a Silhouette

color(s)
need to be fed
by
LIGHT
to have
their color(s)

in

every season

Madness Is a Personal Metaphor
Akhila Pingali

Poetry

NATIONALITY Indian
FIRST LANGUAGE Telugu
SECOND LANGUAGES English & Hindi

Appeared in Issue Fall '22

My body is a tree. So I stand stock-still on the sidewalk wriggling my toes in the dirt. If my head is a wired eyrie, birds are thoughts of prey. Sometimes they come clutching a dead rat, others a kicking sheep. I spin under a bus shelter for better nestling. I tell the mountain trees waiting for the bus I am a vessel that takes the shape of the humours. Tell, don't show, *this is my handle and this is my spout.* There is no space to be a teapot on that government bus. I tell my crockery friends riding with me that I'm separated from my world by a layer of wasp wings so that when I touch my community I'm not actually touching them and when I see them they colour differently. The strangers peer back at me through a cataract over their one conventional eye. When someone flags down the bus I creep over on my bottom and wriggle fluently down the stairs. That's how water would do it, the world's greatest solvent. The irony is, when someone asks for a drink, I am dry. In the kitchen wall above the sink I'm a promontory of sludge-filled steel. That is why my therapist lies on the couch while I protrude from her vision board. She pushes me to narrate, I gurgle and sputter, spitting out muck on her notebook, where it forms words like water on a duck's back. She tells me that poetry is a personal metaphor. Remember this when we talk of cures: A metaphor untranslated could fail an entire language and a unanimous language often fails its instances of poetry. When I hold forth on birds for two hours nonstop, in my head we are all just going *I want to live, I want to live.*

The River
Jingshu Yao

Fiction

NATIONALITY Chinese
FIRST LANGUAGE Mandarin
SECOND LANGUAGE English

Appeared in Issue Fall '19

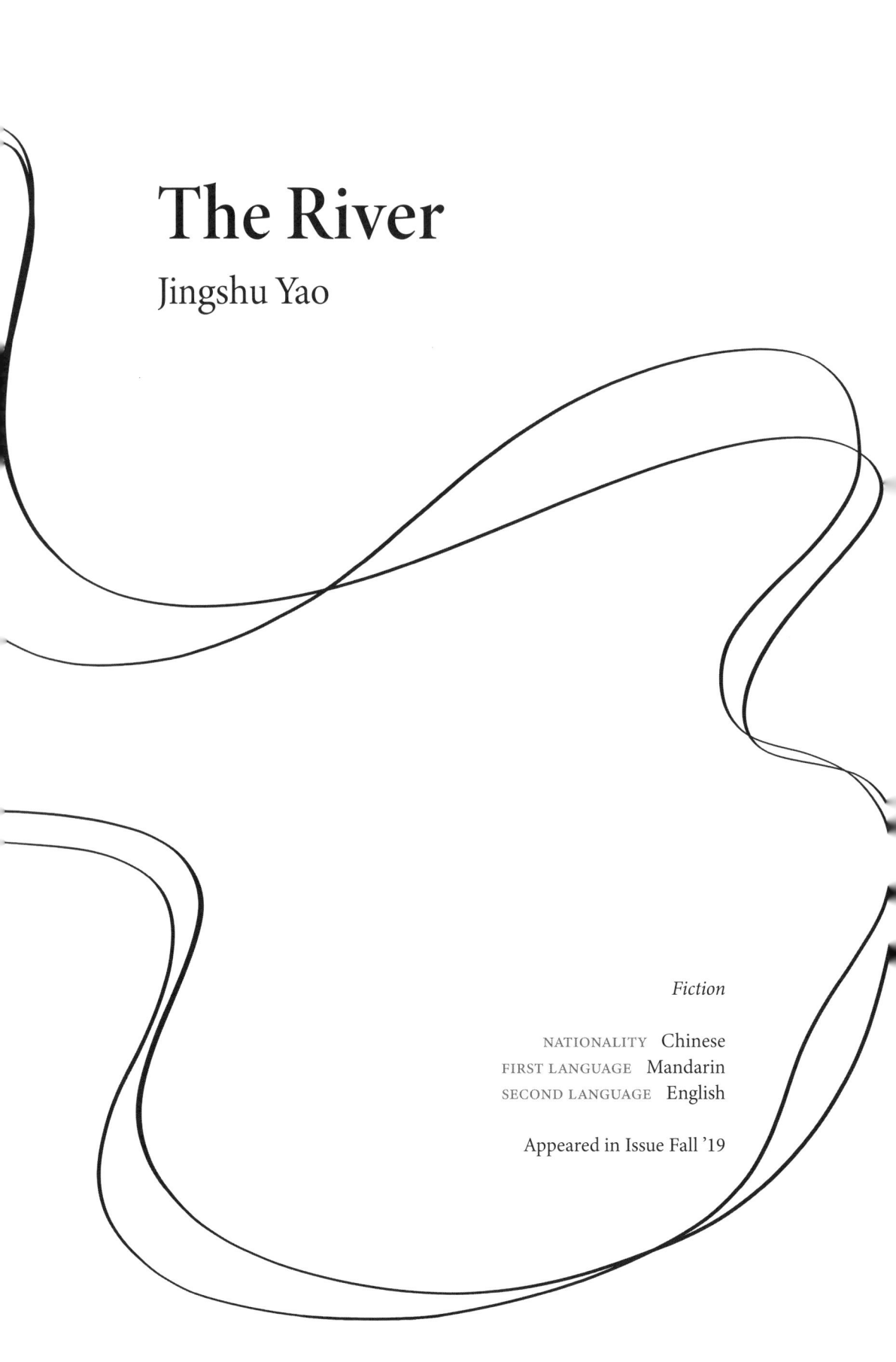

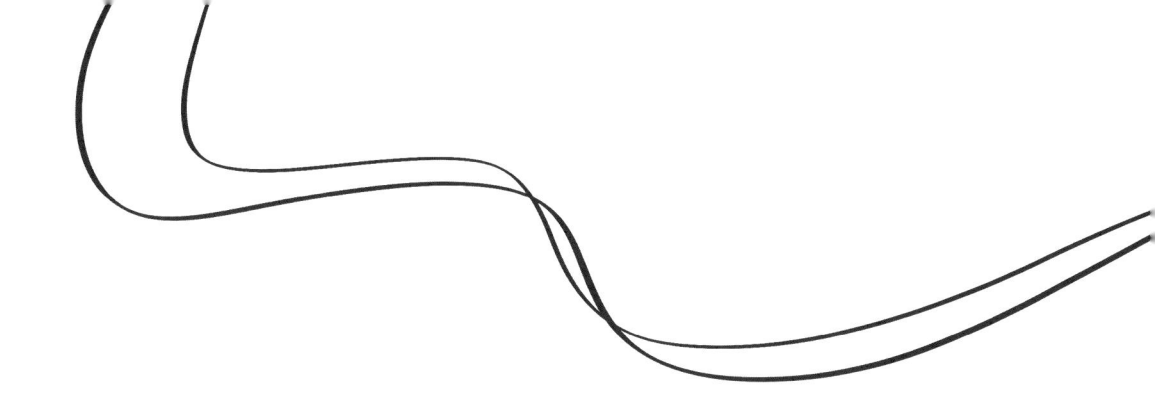

> I wish our hearts were one,
> So the river never ends.
> — Li Zhiyi (1103)

只愿君心似我心
定不负相思意
－李之仪

"Guess what? We are in the same class again! Isn't that great? I never thought I would see a familiar face in middle school." Your voice sounded so excited through the speaker. My hand was shaking the phone slightly. We had been in the same class since grade 3 but never actually close.

We started as a drop of water,
from the ice sheet,
on the top of the mountain.
We traveled on our own,
till the confluence.

You were one of the tall and beautiful girls sitting at the back of the classroom. Coming from Shanghai, where the Yangtze River joins the sea, you had the confidence of a girl from a big city. Teachers adored you, girls admired you, boys wrote love letters and snuck them into your notebooks. I, on the other hand, was a short tomboy sitting in the front row. Boys pulled my hair while I tried to kick their bottoms. I screamed and chased them around, fell onto the dusty ground and tore my clothes. Teachers and parents sighed at the sight of me.

"When will you stop being so childish and start to act like a girl?" Coming from Sichuan for my parents' job commission, I clearly had an accent that didn't belong to the East Coast. I spent my younger years not that far from the Tanggula Mountains, where the glaciers give birth to the spring that later becomes the longest river in China.

A rough muddy brook joined a clear stream.
They merged and went along the creek.

We were as different as the two sides of magnets, the new environment of high school becoming the magnetic field that drew us together. We were the unlikely friends that no one had expected. I felt so lucky to walk with you arm in arm, to sit beside one another in the cafeteria and during the bus ride home, to do our little talks between girls. We talked about the books we read, the shows we watched, your cat and my plants, teachers, classmates, the boy who sat next to you and always made you angry...

When the river bed widened the water slowed down.
The dust and mud sunk and the clear liquid ran.
The future had no limit and life was long.
The creek flowed leisurely with a burbling sound.

I stopped swearing because I couldn't face your amber colored eyes filled with blame. I yelled in public no more for you frowned every time I let my manners slip. I grew my boyish hair to my shoulders and hoped it would be as elegant as yours. I changed thoroughly for you.

The rocks and logs blocked water on its way.
But water couldn't reject,
for the obstacles are in its heart.

Growing up, you became more attractive, changed boyfriends several times; girls crowded by your side but said negative things behind your back. I thought myself as your most loyal friend but there was always someone cooler around you. Great tides were raised in my feelings. Jealousy splashed everywhere when you walked hand in hand with a boyfriend or sat in the center of the girls in the cafeteria. The spray of anger overwhelmed and scared me. I carefully hid my thoughts, fearing that you would distance yourself from me for what was on my mind.

Only fools would attempt to hold the movement of the river.
A fool or someone desperate.

One day on the bus, you told me with excitement that your deskmate, the boy who always made you angry, said that he liked you. This was not your first boyfriend, but you still blushed. Your face lit up, more beautiful than ever.

You whispered, "If one day, you meet someone you like, tell me first, okay?"

I smiled and said nothing. I tried the best a 15-year-old could to maintain my dignity and pride.

The next day you saw me, my hair was above my earlobe again.

The creek kept flowing while the water sang along.

The river joined together but also separated,
they might split to form an island,
or they came to the bifurcation
where the joint journey ended.

"How long since we last met? Three months? Five?"

Six months and a week. I didn't say it out loud because I didn't want you to know that I'd been keeping track of our separated days, one by one.

You were taller, your face had lost the chubby of a girl and grown the charm of a woman. You were still beautiful, but different.

The river left the mountains and ceased to be limited.
With great enthusiasm it ran toward the boundless plain.

The first year after graduation, we were still best friends. We met regularly on the weekends and went on trips together during the summer. We texted each other good night before going to bed, no matter how busy we were. My heart raced every time my phone vibrated and I smiled at the green message box that had your name on it. I had your photos on my lock screen and stared at your face every time I felt down. I kept talking to you, in my head, in my dreams, and in my writing. I could feel your presence during all the days we were separated. You were always with me. I wrote poems for you but never gained enough courage to show them to you. The lines only talked about trees, flowers, birds, and rain but I was afraid that someone as smart and sensitive as you would do well to see through the hints.

With a heavier course load and my parents taking away my cell phone to avoid distractions, we couldn't stay in touch as often. But my mind wandered to you whenever it could.

No one ever steps in the same river twice,
for it's not the same river and one is not the same one.

We talked until our coffee got cold. High school, new people and a new life. You were in Mathletes and got great marks. I was writing a story about spaceships. Once again you were at the top of your class, while my grades rose and fell, like a drifting boat.

You said you didn't like science fiction and you didn't have much time to read because of the heavy schoolwork. You said you needed to get into a good university and that was your focus right now.

The riverbed went on in two different directions.
The water split with a part of one another among each other.

Eventually, you said you were dating a boy from your high school. Tall, handsome, and as smart as you. You were so happy.

"Have you met anybody yet?"

"No, not really." 17 years old was a perfect age to lie, the words slipped out of me without any difficulty.

"I'm sure you will soon. By the way, if you're going to the classmates reunion next week, can you bring this letter to my ex? I don't feel like seeing him."

I held up the piece of paper; it was as thin as a knife.

Water never gets hurt, for you can't cut water open, with any weapons.

The land opened up,
but the bank was steep,
and the watercourse creeps.
It was a long way for the river,
to travel through the meander.

"I'm sorry to wake you up but please listen to me."

You called me at midnight and said that you felt isolated. Nobody around you seemed to understand what you were going through. You went to a university in Chongqing, where the Yangtze is still in its upper course. It's a good school but you didn't want to study what your parents chose and you didn't need your boyfriend to tell you what to do from the other side of the country. You didn't care about what others thought of you anymore; you hated the feeling that you were living a life for someone else.

The river has no fear for water is its heart,
transparency stands for honesty,
shapelessness means invincibility.

I sat on my bed in the dorm of my nameless university located in Suzhou, the last watertown nourished by the Yangtze before it enters the modern craziness of Shanghai. I listened to you talking on and on until you calmed down and said you were fine; you just needed someone to talk to. You asked me if I understood.

"I don't have to understand. I just want to listen."

You remained silent for a long time but neither of us hung up.

"I just don't know if I will ever make some impact, even a tiny little one."

The river leaves no mark, for water has no color or smell,
but the river remembers where it washes through,
and what it washed through remembers the fondle of water.

You already had, in my life. The words were just on the tip of my tongue but I swallowed them down as you started to talk again.

"You know, you're such a good friend. I lost contact with most classmates in middle school. I'm glad that you're not one of them — were you saying anything?"

"You should go back to sleep."
I listened to your light laughter and you said good night.

The river flows away quietly, same as the sleepless night.

The river was a river no more when it entered the sea.
It lost its clearness and took on bitterness and salt.

"You look so different."
    We didn't talk for a whole year before you called again. This time through video so we could see each other. Indeed, I was different and so were you. My hair grew longer again and I had stopped wearing T-shirts and sport pants all year around. I had become mild and gentle again but this time, not for you. Your hair was gold, your lips were red, your eyebrows stretched and darkened, your lashes thickened and lengthened. I looked at you as if you were a stranger.

But the river never regrets,
for all the rivers meet at the sea.

I was happy to see you but the level of excitement and anxiety was not what it used to be. We caught up over WeChat like any old friends would. You broke up with your high school boyfriend and found a new one at university. You said that young love is always silly. You were in an exchange program in Nebraska and I lived in Toronto for one year. You said that Americans are loud and lazy but they provide better education so you have to be there. I liked the diversity and inclusive environment in Canada but my financial situation as an international student troubled me. We talked and laughed. The uneasiness at the sight of you in middle school, the shivering upon hearing your voice over the phone in high school, all the feelings that overwhelmed me every time I thought about you over the years had disappeared. Time changed you as well as me. I entered another stream, one that was more steady and calm.

The river ended.
We eventually met at the sea.

"So what's new?"

"I met someone."

"What's he like?"

I paused. Pride month, rainbow flag, her smile the first time I asked her out. My heart raced as your familiar amber eyes looked through the screen, filled with curiosity. It took a long time for a drop of water to reach the ocean, but it did, eventually.

"She's nice."

You cheered and leaned toward the screen, "I knew it, you like girls. That's so cool, tell me everything!"

I started to talk about my girlfriend while you smiled and listened as I used to do when you described your boyfriends. I met her at a writing circle and exchanged numbers; both aware of the mutual feeling we started dating. It was a rather short story compared to the story that I chose not to tell, the story about you.

More water continued to flow,
tracelessly from mountain to ocean.

"I am so happy for you. How about your writing, are you working on something right now?"

"A poem. A poem about a river."

The river never ended.

Biographies

EDITORS

Filippo Bagnasco has been published twice in the literary issues of *Tint Journal* and he has been working there as a volunteer since 2021. He curates the In Conversation section, a welcoming place for book reviews and author interviews, with an exclusive focus on ESL authors and works. He is also a PhD student at the University of Graz, Austria, where he studies contemporary American fiction, age, and gender. He finds pleasure and solace in words and, in particular, in the English language.

Andrea Färber is a PhD candidate of English and American Studies at the University of Graz, Austria. She researches literature with a particular interest in the representation of climate change in relation to the more-than-human world. When she is not occupied with reading books or writing, she volunteers for *Tint Journal* as assistant editor and social media manager. Besides her love for literature, she also loves to travel the world, explore different cultures, and learn new languages.

Chiara Meitz is a student of English and American Studies at the University of Graz, Austria. Besides her studies, she enjoys reading, writing, and working with books, at the library or at a second-hand bookshop. She was first published in *Tint Journal* with her flash fiction piece "Nothing" in 2020. Currently, she volunteers for Tint as editorial assistant, project assistant and auditor. Whatever the future holds for her, she knows that her life will always be bookish, be it as an editor, librarian, reader, or writer.

Lisa Schantl is the founder and editor-in-chief of *Tint Journal*, and assistant at *treffpunkt sprachen* – Centre for Language, Plurilingualism and Didactics at the University of Graz, Austria, where she also researches translingual literature. In addition, she freelances as cultural organizer and translator. She studied English and American Studies as well as Philosophy at the University of Graz and Montclair State University, New Jersey. Her writings and translations have appeared in *Asymptote, La Piccioletta Barca, manuskripte, Panel Magazine, PubLab, The Hopper, The Normal Review, UniVerse, Versopolis*, and more. She has received various grants and scholarships, most recently the KUNSTRAUM STEIERMARK scholarship for 2023–24.

GUEST EDITORS

Marjorie Agosín is a poet, scholar, human rights activist, and the Andrew Mellon Professor in the Humanities at Wellesley College. She has authored over 80 books of poetry, memoir, novels and prose collections and two young adult novels. Among her honors are the Pura Belpre Award given by the American Library Association for her YA novel *I Lived On Butterfly Hill* and also the Government of Chile gave her the Gabriela Mistral Medal of Honor. Agosín's work has been translated into several languages, among them Albanian, Serbian, Portuguese, Hebrew, and Italian. Her work as an activist has played an important role in her writing life and the United Nations granted a leadership award for her work on behalf of women's rights across the world. Agosín lives on the coast of Maine, the coast of Chile, and in the city of Boston.

Juhea Kim is an author, artist, advocate, and editor of *Peaceful Dumpling*, a sustainable online magazine. Her bestselling debut novel *Beasts of a Little Land* (Ecco) was named a finalist for the 2022 Dayton Literary Peace Prize and a Best Book of 2021 by *Harper's Bazaar*, *Real Simple*, *Ms.*, and *Portland Monthly*. It is being published in thirteen countries around the world, to date. She earned her BA in Art and Archaeology from Princeton University. She is donating a portion of the author proceeds from her novel to the Phoenix Fund, a Siberian tiger and Amur leopard conservation NGO. She is currently working on her second novel and continuing her environmental and animal advocacy in Portland, Oregon.

CONSULTING EDITORS

Matthew Monroy is the prose editor for *Tint Journal*, working out of Plainfield, New Jersey. He is a graduate of Montclair State University where he studied English with a focus on creative writing; this is how he met the team and originally joined as an assistant editor. A lifelong fan of Shakespeare, fantasy, modernist literature, and political journalism, Matthew loves working with

Tint's collective of amazing writers and exploring the cultural roots that make working for Tint so fulfilling. When not working for Tint, Matt is writing his own collection of stories from his childhood. His current writing focus is on unpacking generational trauma and substance abuse, and using writing as a tool for understanding these issues.

John Salimbene is a writer based in the U.S. and has proudly served as the poetry editor for *Tint Journal* since 2019. He holds an MFA from William Paterson University and currently teaches writing at Montclair State University, New Jersey, where the idea for *Tint Journal* first came to fruition. His poems can be found in *Passengers Journal*, *Bodega Magazine*, *Small Orange Journal*, *Voicemail Poems*, and elsewhere.

ART EDITOR

Vanesa Erjavec is a visual artist from Slovenia with a degree in Art History and English Language and Literature. Her work encompasses traditional art and digital illustration, as well as graphic and web design. She explores different art styles, ranging from semi-realism to illustrative dark fantasy. The emphasis is on the duality of human nature; the child-like curiosity and imagination vs. the depth of emotion and expression. She has worked on numerous projects, including design and illustration of books, magazines, websites, the preparation of exhibitions, and as art editor for *Tint Journal*.

AUTHORS

Leila Aboulela's recently published novel, *River Spirit*, was described by *The New York Times* as "dazzling... a novel of war, love, faith, womanhood and — crucially — the tussle over truth and public narratives." Leila's previous novels are *Bird Summons*, *The Kindness of Enemies*, *The Translator*, *Minaret* and *Lyrics Alley*, the latter being the Fiction Winner of the Scottish Book Awards. Her story collection *Elsewhere, Home* won the Saltire Fiction Book of the Year Award. Leila is a winner of the Caine Prize for African Writing, and her work was translated into fifteen languages. She is Honorary Professor of the WORD center at the University of Aberdeen.

Olja Alvir was born in Yugoslavia and grew up in Vienna, where she works as a writer, translator, and literary scholar. She is the author of the German-language novel *Kein Meer* (Zaglossus, 2016) and the trilingual poetry collection *Spielfeld/Špilfeld/Playground* (Kollektiv, 2022), with her poem "Pomelo" winning first prize in a young authors short-form contest in 2021. Her poetry has appeared internationally,

e. g. in *apostrophe*, *Tint Journal*, *Olney Magazine,* and *Kenyon Review*. Alvir has been the recipient of residency fellowships in Split and Zagreb, Croatia. Her literary and political writing on identity and displacement appears in various German-language publications. She is currently pursuing a PhD in South Slavic Literature while working on her second novel.

Natalie Bühler is an emerging writer and arts administrator living on unceded Gadigal Land in Sydney, Australia. She frequently incorporates her native Swiss German, which does not have a standardised written form, into her English writing. Her work has appeared in *Tint Journal*, *Blue Bottle Journal*, and *boats against the current*.

Urvashi Bundel is an award-winning poet and author of *Unapologetically Feminist*, a feminist collection published in March 2022 that explores themes like refugees and women's rights. She received the Poet of the Year 2022 International Literary Award for the same. She is also a humanitarian who has worked at the United Nations High Commissioner for Refugees and the United Nations Office for Project Services. She holds degrees from the Johns Hopkins School of Advanced International Studies and Ritsumeikan Asia Pacific University in Japan, and academic recognitions from Leiden University and Melbourne Law School.

Tim Tim Cheng is a poet and a teacher from Hong Kong, currently based in the UK. Her pamphlet *Tapping At Glass*, which explores girlhood, multilingualism, and psychogeography, is out with Verve in 2023. Her poems are published or anthologised in *POETRY*, *The Rialto*, *Ambit*, *Voice and Verse Poetry Magazine*, and elsewhere. Her latest appearances include the Hidden Door Festival, Singapore Writers Festival, and BBC Scotland. She is a WrICE fellow, a member of Southbank Centre's New Poets Collective 2022/23, and a mentee under the Roddy Lumsden Memorial Mentorship scheme. She edits, translates between Chinese and English, and writes lyrics.

Galina Chernaya was born in Moscow and raised among the Soviet intelligentsia in the Cold War and Brezhnev eras. The daughter of an eminent scientist, she had completed her PhD in Biomechanics and launched a promising research career when she fell afoul of Soviet authorities, culminating in a failed lawsuit against the State for violating the United Nations Universal Declaration of Human Rights. Under threat of imprisonment, she, her husband, and two young children emigrated and were admitted as refugees to the U.S. in 1991. The family settled in Princeton, N. J., where Galina and her husband worked as pharmaceutical scientists. Now living in Vermont, Galina enjoys writing the memoir of her family's struggle and survival. Her first publication, "The Court of the People," appeared serially in *The Evening Street Review* and "Unburying the Past: My Family, the Gulag and Stalin's Secret Police in Ukraine" was recently published in *Cagibi*.

Min "Matthew" Choi is a writer and student in the Writing and Literature program at UC Santa Barbara. He has received the Kieth E. Vineyard Short Story Scholarship and Brancart Fiction Award, and was awarded the Summer Undergraduate Research Fellowship to produce Baek Da-som (and Other Forgotten Names). Min has been published in *Tint Journal*, *Open Ceilings*, and *Catalyst*, and served as a reader and editor for *Spectrum Literary Journal*. He lives in a state between baking and reading, pausing occasionally to write or walk along the beach.

Brianna Colmenares studied Creative Writing at William Paterson University, earning her MFA. She views writing as alchemy, and enjoys including juxtaposing concepts in her work. Her interests also include yoga, astrology, and meditation. Her work has been published in *Tint Journal*.

Lindi Dedek is a writer, poet, filmmaker and clown-in-training from Czechia, currently finishing their MA in Gender Studies. Their fiction writing has appeared in magazines such as *Stadtsprachen*, *Aji Magazine*, and *Lost Boys Press*. They are based in Berlin and love mermaids, black tea, and ballet.

Naoko Fujimoto was born and raised in Nagoya, Japan, and studied at Nanzan Junior College. She was an exchange student and received a BA and MA from Indiana University. Her poetry collections are *We Face the Tremendous Meat on the Teppan*, winner of C&R Press Summer Tide Pool Chapbook Award by C&R Press (2022), *Where I Was Born*, winner of the editor's choice by Willow Books (2019), *GLYPH: graphic poetry = trans. sensory* by Tupelo Press (2021), and four chapbooks. She is a *RHINO* associate & translation editor and *Tupelo Quarterly* translation editor. She is a Bread Loaf Translation scholarship recipient.

Yanita Georgieva is a poet and journalist. She was born in Bulgaria, raised in Lebanon, and now lives in London. In 2022, she received the Out-Spoken Prize for Poetry and was shortlisted for the Ivan Juritz Prize. She is a member of the Southbank New Poets Collective and runs the international poetry collective Dreamboat. You can find her work in *Poetry Wales*, *bath magg*, *Waxwing*, *The Cardiff Review*, and elsewhere.

Lisa Giacalone is a writer based in Germany. She studied English and German literature in Wuppertal and Düsseldorf.

Her main interests lie in poetry and short forms of fiction. She is part of the international writing collective The Rambler.

Edvige Giunta was born and raised in Italy and lives in the United States. She is the author of *Writing with an Accent: Contemporary Italian American Women Authors* and has coedited six anthologies, including *The Milk of Almonds: Italian American Women Writers on Food and Culture* and *Talking to the Girls: Intimate and Political Essays on the Triangle Shirtwaist Factory Fire*. Her writing appears in anthologies, journals, and magazines. A native speaker of Italian, she writes almost exclusively in English, and appreciates the creative potential of porous linguistic borders. She is Professor of English at New Jersey City University.

Viktoriia Grivina is a writer and cultural researcher from Kharkiv, Ukraine. Her personalized essays and short stories focus on social and cultural boundaries, issues of migration, exclusion and borders. She is now working on a debut novel, dedicated to her hometown of Kharkiv, and on a series of humorous stop-motion animations, *Khastoria: Kharkiv Legends*. Her current PhD study at St. Andrews University is dedicated to the mythological and aesthetic transformations of public spaces in Ukraine in times of war.

Jee Ann Guibone is a writer and English teacher from the Philippines. She earned her teaching degree from Xavier University-Ateneo de Cagayan and her Master's degree in Creative Writing from Teesside University. She writes about life in the Philippines, whether it's about the mundane or the macabre — and sometimes, it's a little bit of both.

Wil-Lian Guzmanos is a writing tutor. Her topics of interest include creative writing, teaching, diaspora studies, psychology, arts, and literature. Her work has been published in *Tint Journal* and *Plural: Online Prose Journal*. She was a fellow in the 19th Ateneo National Writers Workshop in 2022.

Gabriela Halas immigrated to Canada during the early 1980s, grew up in northern Alberta, lived in Alaska for seven years, and currently resides in B.C., Canada. She has published poetry in a variety of literary journals, including *The Temz Review*, *Cider Press Review*, *Inlandia*, *About Place Journal*, *Prairie Fire*, *december magazine*, *Rock & Sling*, *Tint Journal*, and *The Hopper*, among others; fiction in *Ruminate*, *The Hopper*, *subTerrain*, *Broken Pencil*, and *en bloc magazine*; nonfiction in *The Whitefish Review*, *Grain*, *Pilgrimage*, *High Country News*, and forthcoming in *Alaska Quarterly Review*. She has received annual Best of the Net nominations in poetry (2020–2022). She lives and writes on Ktunaxa Nation land and is currently completing an MFA at UBC (Vancouver, Canada).

Thea Inuk Lønberg-Jensen is a Danish student working on her MA in English whose passion for books and stories led her to try and create them herself. A dedicated reader and writer in her childhood, she has recently rediscovered her love of the written word. She typically works with darker, melancholic themes, often taking inspiration from her own life as a queer transwoman.

Ioana Morpurgo has published numerous articles on literary and socio-cultural topics in *New Internationalist*, *Contemporary Review*, *Lichtungen*, *Buchkultur*, *Romania literara*, *Dilema veche*, and *Observator Cultural*, among others. She has contributed short prose and essays to anthologies worldwide, such as *The Review of Contemporary Fiction* (2010), *Best of Short Prose 2000* (2013), and *10.000 Characters* (ICR, 2017). She is the author of three novels: *Fișă de înregistrare* (*Record Slip* — Polirom, 2004), *Imigrantii* (*The Immigrants* — Polirom, 2011) and *Schije* (*Shrapnel* — Polirom, 2017), and the curator of "Airborne Particles," a renga poem exploring the state of isolation during lockdown, involving 100 poets worldwide. Morpurgo is based in the UK and a member of the Romanian Union of Writers, of PEN Club Romania, and of the Green Party UK.

Leonid Newhouse wrote about his experience growing up in the former Soviet Union in *The Fairytale House*, a manuscript for which he received the 1998–99 Writing Fellowship from the Memorial Foundation for Jewish Culture. His work has been published in *JewishFiction.net*, *Tint Journal*, *Maggid: A Journal of Jewish Literature*, and, most recently, in *The Westchester Review*.

Sihle Ntuli, a poet from Durban, South Africa, is a recipient of the 2023 Johannesburg Institute for Advanced Studies Writing Fellowship for his poetry. His work has been featured in leading journals such as *Frontier Poetry*, *SAND Journal*, and *Herri & Mizna*, amongst others. He is the author of the chapbooks *Rumblin* (uHlanga, 2020) and *The Nation* (River Glass Books, 2023).

Adriana Onițǎ is a poet, artist, educator, and researcher with a PhD in Education. Her poems appear on the 2021 CBC Poetry Prize Shortlist, in *The Globe and Mail*, in her chapbook *Conjugated Light* (Glass Buffalo, 2019), and in the Romanian Women Voices in North America series. She is the founding editor of *The Polyglot* and the editorial director of the Griffin Poetry Prize.

Yuko Otomo is a visual artist and a bilingual (Japanese/English) writer of Japanese origin. She writes poetry, haiku, art criticism, travelogues, and essays. Her publications include *Garden: Selected Haiku* (Beehive Press, 2000), *STUDY & Other Poems on Art* (Ugly Duckling Presse, 2013), *FROZEN HEATWAVE*, a collaborative linked poem project with Steve Dalachinsky (Luna Bisonte Prods, 2017), *anonymous landscape* (Lithic Press, 2019), *In Delacroix's Garden*, a collaborative book with Basil King (Spuyten Duyvil, 2022) and the most recent *PINK* (Lithic Press), due in 2023. She lives in New York City.

Gladwell Pamba is a Kenyan writer whose fictional works explore humour and escapism as coping mechanisms. She is the recipient of the inaugural CC Adetula Fellowship 2023, Jahazi Press Masterclass, and UEA/Goethe Masterclass by Tsitsi Dangarembga. She was the East Africa winner at the International Literary Festival 2022 and the AFREADA winner 2019. Her stories have been nominated for Best of the Net, Sondeka Awards, and Writivism Prize in 2019. Her works have been anthologized while others appear in *Bakwa Magazine*, *Iskanchi Press*, *The Offing*, *Waxwing Literary Journal*, *A Long House*, *Five South Journal*, *Tint Journal*, *Patchwork*, *Kikwetu Journal*, and elsewhere.

Susmita Paul is an Indian bilingual writer. She is the second prize winner of the Grazer Poesieautomaten project's 50-Cent-Preis. Her works in Bengali and in English have been published in *Kaurab*, *Tint Journal*, *Through the Looking Glass: Reflecting on Madness and Chaos Within*, *Saaranga*, *The New Amrita Bazar Patrika*, *Poetry and Covid*, and others. She is the editor-in-chief of *The Pine Cone Review*. She is also a Zentangle-inspired artist and leads creative writing workshops. She is currently working on a grief-themed manuscript.

Giada Pesce has been writing poetry since she was 11. She is an Italian multidisciplinary artist based in Hamburg, Germany. She ran the poetry performances "The Dip of Salt into Water" (Hamburg 2019/2020), collaborated with art magazine *Patricide* (Dark Window Press, 2011/2012), the daily magazine of the 23rd edition of the Turin Film Festival (2005), and the Italian magazine *Filmaker's magazine* (2005). She worked as a translator for the film *Il Sud è niente* by Fabio Mollo, for Achille Bonito Oliva's *Enciclopedia della Parola*, and his appendix on Carlo Giulio Argan's *Modern Art*.

Akhila Pingali is a research scholar and translator based in Hyderabad, India. Her work has appeared in *SoFloPoJo*, *trampset*, *Defunkt Magazine*, *Five Minutes*, *Brave Voices Magazine*, *Tint Journal*, *Contemporary Literary Review India*, and in an anthology called *Ninety-Seven Poems*.

Skanda Prasad grew up in Bangalore, India and moved to Atlanta, U.S., to study Electrical Engineering at Georgia Tech. He received the Thomas Lux Poetry Award in 2018. His PhD research involves developing radars that can image highly maneuverable objects. He wishes his cooking was as good as he thinks it is.

Francisco Serrano is a queer immigrant residing in New York City, who uses poetry and photography as storytelling tools. Whether a candid or a staged portraiture, their top priority is to create palpable imagery, which also applies to their writing. What started as random fun four years ago has grown to taking the opportunity in letting the world hear what they have to say.

Nilofar Shidmehr is a bilingual writer, poet, research-creation scholar, and educator. She is the author of two collections of short fiction and five books of poetry in English and Persian. Her first English poetry book, *Shirin and Salt Man*, was nominated for a British Columbia Book Prize. Her latest collection of short fiction, *Divided Loyalties*, has received many positive reviews. She has served three times as a Writer in Residence in different cities in Canada. She teaches creative writing and courses in history, literature and cinema of modern Iran at Douglas College and in the Continuing Education Program at Simon Fraser University.

Ilan Stavans is an internationally renowned, award-winning essayist, translator, cultural critic, poet, and editor. He is Lewis-Sebring Professor of Humanities and Latin American and Latino Culture at Amherst College, the publisher of *Restless Books*, and a consultant to the Oxford English Dictionary. He has translated Sor Juana Ines de la Cruz, Jorge Luis Borges, Pablo Neruda, and Juan Gelman into English, Emily Dickinson and Elizabeth Bishop into Spanish, Isaac Bashevis Singer from Yiddish, Yehuda Halevi and Yehuda Amichai from Hebrew, and *Don Quixote de la Mancha*, *The Little Prince*, and *Alice in Wonderland* into Spanglish. His work has been adapted into film, TV, theater, and radio. Among his many books are *On Borrowed Words: A Memoir of Language* (2001), *Dictionary Days: A Defining Passion* (2008), and *The People's Tongue: Americans and the English Language* (2023).

Laura Theis' writing appears in *Poetry*, *Mslexia*, *Magma*, and *Rattle*, among others. Her Elgin-Award-nominated debut *how to extricate yourself*, an Oxford Poetry Library Book-of-the-Month, won the Brian Dempsey Memorial Prize. She received the AM Heath Prize, EAL Oxford Brookes Poetry Prize, Mogford Prize, Hammond House International Literary Award, and a Forward Prize nomination. Shortlisted for the Women Poets' Prize and the Bridport Prize, she was a finalist for the National

Poetry Competition, BBC Short Story Award, and the Alpine Fellowship. Her forthcoming book *A Spotter's Guide To Invisible Things* won the Live Canon Collection Prize and was selected for the Arthur Welton Award by the Society of Authors.

Maja Ulasik holds two Master's degrees in Scandinavian Studies and in Anglophone Literatures. In 2022, her MA thesis on the theme of trauma healing through reconnection to nature in Native American literature was recognized with the MUMA Award. Her poetry and short stories have been published, among others, in *Popshot Magazine*, *Tint Journal,* and *Brussels City of Stories Magazine*. Recently, she has begun writing her debut novel, an excerpt of which she performed in the last edition of the Asmara Addis Literary Festival in Brussels. In her free time, she works as a volunteer language teacher for refugees. She lives in Brussels.

Jingshu Yao was born and raised in Nanjing, China, and is now based in Toronto. She holds an MA in Museum Studies from the University of Toronto and works as a program coordinator at Heritage Toronto. Jingshu's writings focus on the intersectionality of identities, the theme of food, immigration, language, and queerness. She is currently working on a novel project about family, secrets, and self-exploration.

Huina Zheng holds a MA in English Studies and works as a college essay coach. She serves as an associate editor for *Bewildering Stories*. Her stories were published in *Baltimore Review*, *Variant Literature*, *Midway Journal*, *Tint Journal*, and others. Her fiction "Ghost Children" was nominated for the Pushcart Prize. She lives in Guangzhou, China, with her husband and daughter.

Tint Writers

Tint Journal would not exist if it were not for all the ESL writers who chose to publish their work with our magazine. Here we want to acknowledge them, from the first to the tenth issue, from Spring '19 to Fall '23, including this anthology:

Eric Abalajon *Leila Aboulela* Rimona Afana *Nafisa A. Iqbal* Chotiya Ahuja *Eneida P. Alcalde* E. Izabelle Cassandra Alexander *Olja Alvir* Maria Arango *Cristaly Lorraine Argenal* J.T. Aris *Eniola Abdulroqeeb Arówólò* Nazli Artemia *Khem K. Aryal* Heike Auer *Ifeoluwa Ayandele* Filippo M. Bagnasco *Joelle Ballonzoli* Alla Barsukova *Aysel K. Basci* Lissa Batista *Lucy Braun* Arno Bohlmeijer *Conny Borgelioen* Martina Braunegger *Natalie Bühler* Urvashi Bundel *Taslim Burkowicz* Ana Bustelo *Schlomo Cabrera* Sara Siddiqui Chansarkar *Tim Tim Cheng* Galina Chernaya *Richard M. Cho* Min "Matthew" Choi *M.M. Coelho* Brianna Colmenares *Catherine C. Con* Edith Cook *Isabella Cruz Pantoja* Catia Dawood *Christina Dax* Lindi Dedek *Pragya Dhiman* Margreet Dietz *Nikola Dimitrov* Annick Duignan *Ema Dumitriu* Loic Ekinga *Margarita Beatriz Escobar* Andrea Färber *Ella Felber* Italo Ferrante *Giulia Ottavia Frattini* Kaori Fujimoto *Naoko Fujimoto* Charlotte Gajek *Elvis A. Galasinao Jr.* Rosa Angelica Garcia *Valeria García Origel* Yanita Georgieva *David Gev* Sejal Ghia *Lisa Giacalone* Edvige Giunta *Norbert Góra* Sofia Grishchuk *Margo Gritt* Viktoriia Grivina *Ansel Guarneros* Jee Ann Guibone *Brinda Gulati* Satvik Gupta *Lázaro Gutiérrez* Wil-Lian Guzmanos *Ida Hagen* Gabriela Halas *Melanie Hyo-In Han* Benedict Hangiriza *Volha Hapeyeva* Seher Hashmi *Julia Hausstätter* Chengru He *Ana Henriques Brotas* David Herbst *Arantxa Hernandez* Aiden Heung *Karla Hirsch* Walter W. Hölbling *Maria A. Ioannou* Darshita Jain *Douglas Jern* Ranjana Joshi *Natascha Jurácsik* S.A. Karpukhin *Jayant Kashyap* Yael Kastel *Volha Kastsiuk* Lady Key *Maliha Khan* Heidi Kofler *Priyanka Kole* Phyllis C. Koppel *Zosia Koptiuch* Emily Kossak *Nastya Kovalchuk* Herman Kringlund *Caroline Kuba* Selene Lacayo *Matea Lacmanović* Marlene

Lahmer *SaraSwoti Lamichhane* Laetitia Lesieure Desbrière Batista *Dai Lin* Yannis Lobaina *Daniel Loebl* Thea Inuk Lønberg-Jensen *Chanlee Luu* Gershom Gerneth Mabaquiao *Marlena Maduro Baraf* Alexandra Magearu *Sami Mahroum* Maria Makrovasili *Rhea Malik* Davide Mana *Ethel Maqeda* Mario Marčinko *Margit Marenich* Letizia Mariani *Mari-Carmen Marín* Camilla Marotta *Ramon Martensen* Chiara Maxia *Lara Mayr* Chiara Meitz *Constance Mello* Eva Michely *Fezeka Mkhabela* Darsana Mohan *Jan Mohn* Jael Montellano *Johanna Montilla* Giulia Moriconi *Ioana Morpurgo* Hader Morsy *Héctor Muiños* Gabriel Mundo *Ketina Muringaniza* Marcus Narvaez *Chourouq Nasri* George Nevgodovskyy *Leonid Newhouse* Oana Nicola *Bianca-Olivia Nita* Sihle Ntuli *Réka Nyitrai* oβlĩque/o *Daniel Ogba* Adriana Oniță *Yuko Otomo* Gladwell Pamba *Timea Pap* Melania Paszek *Mandira Pattnaik* Susmita Paul *Anika Pavel* Karolina Pawlik *Sergii Pershyn* Giada Pesce *Serena Piccoli* Akhila Pingali *L. E. Pinto* Amalia Pistilli *Carlos A. Pittella* Tatyana Platonova *J.B. Polk* Skanda Prasad *Daniela Rafalt* Ranjiet *Samiksha Tulika Ransom* Neha Rayamajhi *Angela Regius* Frederick Reinprecht *Helia S. Rethmann* Richard Risemberg *Ines Rodrigues* Zoë S. Roy *Sunday T. Saheed* Federica Santini *Saumya Sawant* Gamze S. Saymaz *Philipp Scheiber* Oindri Sengupta *Francisco Serrano* Hibah Shabkhez *Ailun Shi* Nilofar Shidmehr *Leyla Shukurova* Bianca Skrinyar *Nanna A. Skriver* Remi Skytterstad *Caroline Smadja* Johan Smits *Joris Soeding* Leah Soeiro Nentis *Ilan Stavans* Philip Steiner *Lisa Süss* Patrick Sylvain *Frieda Temper* Laura Theis *Iva Ticic* Aydée Tirado *Tjizembua Tjikuzu* Elena Traina *Trang NP Tran* Ilias Tsagas *Yulia Tseytlin* Mandy Moe Pwint Tu *Maja Ulasik* Tatia Veikkola *Lyde Gerard Villanueva* Wambui Waldhauser *David Weber* Anya Weimann *J.M. Wong* Jingshu Yao *Lorna Ye* Changming Yuan *N.M.A. Zambrano* Bänoo Zan *Roya Zendebudie* Hantian Zhang *Huina Zheng* Nikola Živković Takšev

Tint Volunteers

The Tint project is built on the beliefs and efforts of several volunteers. The individuals mentioned in the following list have contributed to Tint in various ways and at various times, and many of them are still deeply involved in this multifaceted endeavor.

Heike Auer *Filippo Bagnasco* Amandine Bourse *Vaniele Casimir* Vanessa Cervini *Sandra Chiritescu* Bianca Cosar *Candice Louisa Daquin* Ashish Dwivedi *Vanesa Erjavec* Andrea Färber *Rachel Farr* Valeria García Origel *Maddi Gnewski* Kenneth Guay *Antonia Hafner* Tobias Leitner *Rongqian Ma* Verity Marques *Chiara Meitz* Nermine Mohamed *Matthew Monroy* Claudia Ofner *Claudia Lorraine Rumson* John Salimbene *Lisa Schantl* Sandra Tanzmeister *Anam Tariq* Trang NP Tran *David Weber*

Kickstarter Campaign Backers

We want to thank everyone who supported this book by backing our Kickstarter crowdfunding campaign:

A. Heiling   *Abu Abdul-Quader*   Alexandra Majer   *Allison Rogovin*   Anja Krobath   *Anja Schmedler*   Anna Maria Bartens   *Annick Duignan*   Barbara Seidl   *Bridgette M. Findley*   Carol Rogovin   *Carolina Verrini Lenzi*   Chiara   *Christina Egger*   Corina Meitz   *The Creative Fund by BackerKit*   crovi   *Dagmar Wallenstorfer*   Danijel Mom   *David Herbst*   Diana Leite   *Dina M.*   Dolores   *Elena Traina*   Elias   *Emilia Bagnasco*   Fabia Fuchs   *H.*   Hannah Drobir   *Heidemarie Kofler*   Holly Kuyper   *Huina Zheng*   Inge Wallage   *Irene Yoon*   Jakob Erhard   *Janice Rogovin*   Jasmin Haselsteiner-Scharner   *Jonathan Aders*   Josef Kirchner   *Juliana Wambui Waldhauser*   Karin & Klaus   *Kismet Biasi*   Klara   *Lea Schönet*   Lisa   *Lisa Jeusch*   Lisa Ziermann   *Luggi*   Mackenzie   *Marcel Masten*   Mario Kolli   *Mario Müller*   Martina Braunegger   *Max Hirschbäck*   Michael Postmann   *MojoExMachina*   Natalie   *Nikola Dimitrov*   Oliver Gajek   *Pavao*   Ralf Pfau   *Richard Cho*   Richard Zangl   *the Rogovin family*   Ronja A. P.   *S. Chen*   Sandra   *Shifra Steinberg*   SimonC.   *Stephen Quann*   Sybil Collas   *the Trojan family*   Trude and Othmar Schantl   *Ulli*   Wolfgang Windisch   *Yannis Lobaina*

Special thanks goes to the backers who also purchased a gift copy for a public library or social association:

Allison Rogovin   *Chiara*   Corina Meitz   *Emilia Bagnasco*   Jasmin Haselsteiner-Scharner   *Jonathan Aders*   Karin & Klaus   *Luggi*   Pavao   *Trude and Othmar Schantl*   Wolfgang Windisch

Content Warnings

Can You See? by Thea Inuk Lønberg-Jensen (p. 196)
    transphobia
Coty 24 by Jee Ann Guibone (p. 186)
    corpse, emotional & physical abuse, homophobia, mentions of death, mentions of substance abuse
Dogs by Giada Pesce (p. 66)
    abuse, animal cruelty, blood
Evenings in Monroe Apartments by Gladwell Pamba (p. 134)
    child abandonment, loss
For Your Own Good by Huina Zheng (p. 150)
    child abuse, emotional & physical abuse, mentions of death, violence
Hard Labor: Childbirth Soviet Style by Galina Chernaya (p. 110)
    childbirth, abuse, trauma
History Flooding the Continent by Ioana Morpurgo (p. 90)
    blood, death, displacement
How We Said Goodbye by Yanita Georgieva (p. 130)
    burial, loss
Immigrant Sitcom by Francisco Serrano (p. 92)
    classism, racism
Into Something Rich and Strange by Lisa Giacalone (p. 132)
    death
It's Like a Curry Sandwich by Skanda Prasad (p. 68)
    mentions of colonialism, mentions of religious hate
jailmaze by Maja Ulasik (p. 146)
    confinement
Madness Is a Personal Metaphor by Akhila Pingali (p. 206)
    mental health

My Azov Sea by Viktoriia Grivina (p. 32)
   mentions of kidnapping, mentions of violence, war
No Place Called Home by Urvashi Bundel (p. 82)
   abuse, death, displacement, mentions of rape, racism, violence
Snake Baby by Min "Matthew" Choi (p. 120)
   blood, mentions of death, substance abuse
Still Life with Deer by Wil-Lian Guzmanos (p. 40)
   death, loss, mentions of war crimes, violence
The Hijab as a Red Herring by Leila Aboulela (p. 168)
   religious hate, sexual harassment
The Liars' Village by Lindi Dedek (p. 24)
   childhood trauma, mentions of abuse, mentions of illness, neglect, substance abuse
The Overcoat by Leonid Newhouse (p. 48)
   classism, mentions of domestic violence
The River-Song by Susmita Paul (p. 138)
   displacement, loss, mentions of death, natural disaster
The Singing Tree by Nilofar Shidmehr (p. 96)
   discrimination, eating disorders, loneliness, racism
Three Chairs by Naoko Fujimoto (p. 128)
   mentions of death, war
Two Possibilities for Shylock by Ilan Stavans (p. 142)
   antisemitism, classism, religious hate
When We First Arrived, 1983 by Gabriela Halas (p. 86)
   classism, discrimination

List of Illustrations

SECTION ARTWORK

15	BELONGING	**The Full Moon Hangs** by Μαρία Καραγεωργίου
77	(IM)MIGRATION	**What Remains of Us** by Lal Buraans
105	UPHEAVAL	**Angst** by Suzette Dushi
163	IDENTITIES	**Sunny Day in a Park** by Alida Ozolina

STORY ARTWORK

All prose and poetry illustrations by Vanesa Erjavec

Endnotes

1. Dembeck, Till. "Sprache und Kultur." In: Till Dembeck and Rolf Parr, eds. *Literatur und Mehrsprachigkeit: Ein Handbuch*. Tübingen: Narr Francke Attempto Verlag, 2020, p. 21.
2. Ette, Ottmar. *Writing-Between-Worlds: TransArea Studies and the Literatures-Without-A-Fixed-Abode*. Trans. Vera M. Kutzinski. Boston: De Gruyter, 2016, p. xxii.
3. According to an *Ethnologue* estimate, see Lyons, Dylan. "How Many People Speak English, And Where Is It Spoken?" *Babbel Magazine*, https://www.babbel.com/en/magazine/how-many-people-speak-english-and-where-is-it-spoken. Accessed 26 Sept. 2023.
4. Crystal, David. *English as a Global Language*. 2nd edition. Cambridge: Cambridge University Press, 2003, pp. 29, 59.
5. Cabrera, Isabel. "World Reading Habits in 2021 [Infographic]." *GLOBALEnglishEditing*, 2021, https://geediting.com/world-reading-habits-in-2021-infographic/. Accessed 11 Sept. 2023.
6. Holifield, Chris. "The English Language Publishing World." *Writers Services*, https://www.writersservices.com/resources/english-language-publishing-world-inside-publishing/. Accessed 26 Sept. 2023.
7. Probyn, Elspeth. *Outside Belongings*. London: Routledge, 1995, p. 19.
8. Anderson, Benedict. *Imagined Communities*. London: Verso, 1983, p. 6.
9. Simic, Charles. "Foreword" in *American Odysseys: Writings by New Americans*. London: Dalkey Archive Press, 2013, p. 22.
10. Danticat, Edwige. *Create Dangerously: The Immigrant Writer at Work*. Princeton: Princeton University Press, 2012, p. 112.
11. Caruth, Cathy. *Unclaimed Experience: Trauma, Narrative, and History*. Baltimore: Johns Hopkins Press, 1996, p. 4.

12 Balaev, Michelle. "Trends in Literary Trauma Theory." *Mosaic: An Interdisciplinary Critical Journal*, vol. 41, no. 2 (2008), p. 150.
13 Pederson, Joshua. "Speak, Trauma: Toward a Revised Understanding of Literary Trauma Theory." *Narrative*, vol. 22, no. 3 (2014), p. 349.
14 Traumatic memories may be altered as a spatial and temporal distortion is likely to occur. (Pederson 349)
15 Balaev. "Trends," pp. 160–163.
16 Bamberg, Michael. "Identity and Narration." In: Peter Hühn, Jan Christoph Meister, John Pier & Wolf Schmid, eds. *Handbook of Narratology*. Boston: De Gruyter, 2014, pp. 241–252.
17 see de Courtivron, Isabelle, ed. *Lives in Translation: Bilingual Writers on Identity and Creativity*. New York: Palgrave Macmillan, 2003.